STAR ATTRACTION
BULLETIN
BOARDS

Shereen Gertel Rutman

Troll Associates

Interior Illustrations by: Marilyn Barr

ISBN: 0-8167-2590-X

Printed in the United States of America.

10 9 8 7 6 5 4 3

CONTENTS

The classroom environment makes a noticeable difference in the way children feel about school. The arrangement of the furniture, the accessibility of materials, the wall displays and decorations—all this influences how children learn and how they interact with one another and with the classroom materials. Displaying the children's work emphasizes that it is a valuable, important part of the classroom environment, and you should place as much of it on a bulletin board as possible. This book offers ideas for eighty-four different bulletin boards, which are made through a cooperative effort between you and the children. As you work through the directions for the bulletin boards, always remember that the process of creating is more important than the final product.

ART MATERIALS TO COLLECT

The bulletin-board ideas suggest using various art media, most of which are common school supplies or art materials. Others are ''found'' materials that children can help you gather throughout the school year. Following is a list of materials that you might want to collect, save, and use during the year.

PAPER

- mural paper
- construction paper
- writing paper
- tagboard
- white paper
- sentence strip paper
- index cards
- tissue paper
- chart paper

MARKERS

- crayons
- magic markers
- chalk
- paint
- pencils

FOOD

- apples
- potatoes
- food coloring
- eggshells
- fruits with seeds

ADHESIVES AND TAPES

- glue
- transparent tape
- masking tape
- tacks
- stapler
- pins
- brass fasteners

COLLAGE MATERIALS

- Styrofoam meat trays
- Styrofoam peanuts
- pipe cleaners
- fabric scraps
- wallpaper books
- buttons
- feathers
- yarn
- ribbon
- burlap
- craft sticks

SCHOOL SUPPLIES

- paper cutter
- hole punch
- ruler/yardstick (meterstick)
- scissors
- paintbrushes
- water containers
- darning needles
- paint rollers

MISCELLANEOUS

- photographs
- magazines
- newspapers
- leaves
- hairspray
- circus programs
- maps
- book covers
- chicken bones
- dinosaur pictures

Getting to Know You

These self-portrait collages provide a way for children to get to know one another while expressing their individuality. The more interesting the collage materials, the more the children can let their imaginations run free.

 Ray has black curly hair.

 Jason likes to play baseball.

 Marsha wears bows in her hair.

 Roberta likes to play volleyball.

 José likes to ride his bike.

Materials

tagboard or cardboard	glue
yarn	fabric scraps
buttons	crayons
scissors	bulletin-board letters

Directions

1. Distribute tagboard or cardboard and crayons to children and ask them to draw pictures of themselves. Encourage them to let the pictures tell about the things they like to do. For example, one child may draw himself riding a bike; another child may show herself playing checkers.

2. Give children yarn, fabric scraps, buttons, other collage materials, scissors, and glue. Invite them to embellish their pictures by adding "yarn" hair, "clothing," and other details.

3. You may wish to have younger children dictate sentences about themselves. Older children may write a few sentences.

4. Hang the finished self-portraits on the bulletin board. Above their work, hang bulletin-board letters that read "Getting to Know You."

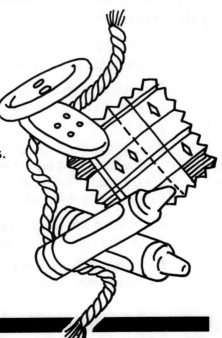

Birthday Graph

This simple bar graph is a fine way to help children get to know one another and to learn about reading graphs. You can leave this birthday chart up all year and refer to it as each child's birthday occurs. The children will enjoy discussing which month has the most birthdays, who is the oldest and the youngest in the class, and who has birthdays on the same day, in the same week, or in the same month.

Materials

mural paper   glue
bulletin-board letters   crayons
construction paper   ruler
scissors   stapler

Directions

1. Hang the mural paper on the bulletin board and use a ruler to divide it into twelve equal columns.

2. Glue or staple bulletin-board letters for the names of the month, from September through August, to the tops of the columns.

3. Use the construction paper and the pattern on page 91 to trace and cut out a person for each child. Encourage children to use crayons to decorate their "people" to resemble themselves.

4. Have children write their names and the dates of their birth on their cutouts.

5. Invite children to glue their cutouts in the column that shows the month of their birth.

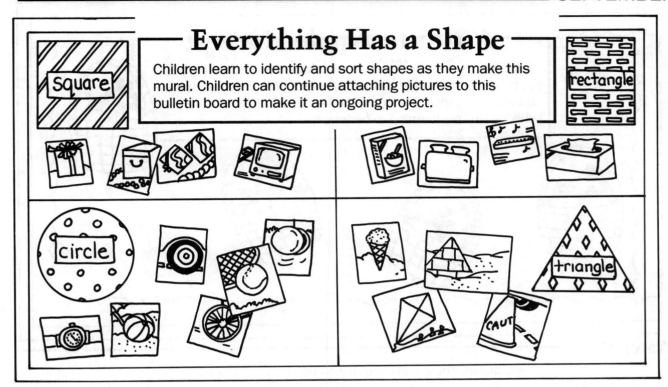

Everything Has a Shape

Children learn to identify and sort shapes as they make this mural. Children can continue attaching pictures to this bulletin board to make it an ongoing project.

Materials

magazines   glue

scissors   markers

mural paper   ruler

construction paper

Directions

1. Using a ruler, divide the mural paper into four equal boxes.

2. Cut out a square, circle, triangle, and rectangle from construction paper.

3. Glue one shape at the top of each box and write the corresponding shape word inside it.

4. Place the mural paper on an art table or on the floor.

5. Discuss the different shapes with children. Ask them to look through old magazines to find objects with these shapes.

6. Have children cut out pictures and glue them in the appropriate boxes.

7. After each child has worked on the mural and the glue has dried, hang the mural on the bulletin board. Once the mural is hung, children can add pictures if there is room.

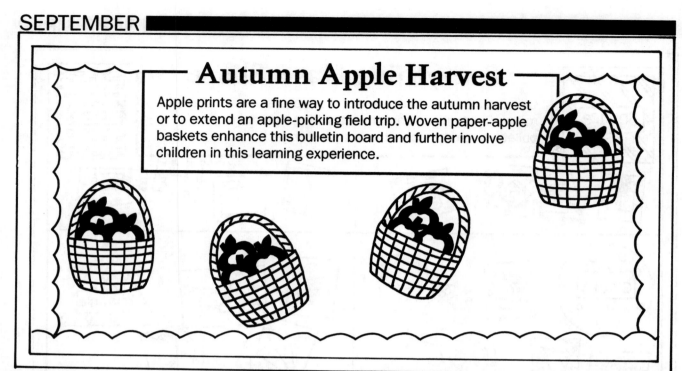

Autumn Apple Harvest

Apple prints are a fine way to introduce the autumn harvest or to extend an apple-picking field trip. Woven paper-apple baskets enhance this bulletin board and further involve children in this learning experience.

Materials

red, brown, and green construction paper

mural paper

apples cut in half

scissors

white paint

stapler

Directions

1. Cover the bulletin board with mural paper.

2. Cut half of the brown construction paper into 1-inch (2 1/2-cm) strips.

3. Cut the rest of the brown paper in the following manner. Bend the shorter side over to create a 1-inch (2 1/2-cm) fold. From the opposite end of the paper cut 1-inch (2 1/2-cm) strips up to the fold.

4. Show children how to weave the strips by alternating the over-and-under pattern for each row. When the woven mats are complete, bend the edges to make them look like baskets. Tape or paste the edges to secure them.

5. Cut apple shapes out of the red paper and leaves out of the green paper. Cut handles out of the brown paper.

6. Dip the apple halves in paint, wiping away any excess. Press the painted apple onto the apple cutout to get an apple print.

7. When the apple prints dry, fit them and the leaves into the baskets and staple them to the bulletin board.

Find Your Name

This engaging bulletin board is a fine way to start off the school year. It invites children to participate in solving a class puzzle as they learn one another's names.

Materials

mural paper   ruler
chart paper   markers
pencil   stapler

Directions

1. Hang the mural paper on the bulletin board.

2. Write each child's first name in a column on the chart paper.

3. Staple this list to the left side of the bulletin board.

4. Using a pencil and a ruler, make a grid large enough to contain all of the children's names and some additional letters.

5. Using a marker, write each child's name horizontally, vertically, or diagonally in the grid. After all the names are on the grid, fill in the empty spaces with additional letters.

6. As children arrive in school, encourage them to find and ring their names.

Curious George Wants to Know What You Are Curious About

After reading the classic story *Curious George*, children will delight in recalling George's adventures. Using yellow hat cutouts, invite children to tell what they are curious about.

Materials

brown, yellow, and white construction paper

mural paper

bulletin-board letters

scissors

stapler

markers

crayons

Directions

1. Hang the mural paper on the bulletin board.

2. Use the pattern on page 92 and yellow construction paper to make enough yellow hats for the class. Make a cutout of Curious George (or use the book or an illustration for display).

3. Use markers to add features to the Curious George cutout. Hang the cutout at the top of the bulletin board.

4. Beside Curious George, hang up bulletin-board letters that read "Curious George Wants to Know."

5. Cut a speech bubble out of white construction paper and write "What are you curious about?" on the paper. Staple this beside the cutout of Curious George.

6. After a discussion about Curious George and curiosity, distribute the yellow hat cutouts and crayons. Encourage children to draw on them and write what they are curious about.

7. Staple the hats to the bulletin board at interesting angles.

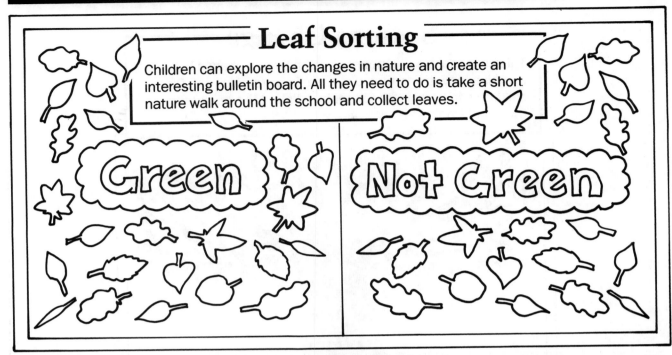

Leaf Sorting

Children can explore the changes in nature and create an interesting bulletin board. All they need to do is take a short nature walk around the school and collect leaves.

Green

Not Green

Materials

mural paper

clear adhesive paper

leaves collected from a nature walk

trays

markers

scissors

ruler

Directions

1. Hang the mural paper on the bulletin board and, using a ruler, divide it into two sections. Write the word *Green* on one side of the paper and the words *Not Green* on the other.

2. Take children on a nature walk in the neighborhood. Let them collect and discuss the different colors of the leaves. Encourage them to talk about the change in seasons and how leaves change color.

3. Have children spread their leaves on trays.

4. Invite each child to choose a leaf and place it facedown on a piece of clear adhesive paper. Cut loosely around the leaf so that there is enough adhesive for it to stick to the bulletin board.

5. Ask children to decide whether their leaves belong in the "Green" group or in the "Not Green" group. Then have them press their leaves onto the appropriate side of the bulletin board to make a beautiful, seasonal leaf collage.

Seasons Change

This seasonal bulletin board gives children a chance to examine leaves and then use them in a creative way. Older children can participate further by painting the trunk of their own "autumn tree."

Materials

mural paper

red, orange, yellow, and brown paint

pencil

paintbrushes

leaves

Directions

1. With a pencil, draw the outline of a large tree on the mural paper.

2. Paint the tree trunk brown or invite children to do so. Let the paint dry.

3. Ask each child to paint the back of a leaf with any of the autumn colors. The leaf should have only a thin layer of paint on it, and the veins should be visible.

4. Have children place the painted sides of their leaves near branches on the tree. Make sure that they press on the unpainted sides to make their leaf prints. After several seconds they can remove their leaves to reveal beautiful prints.

5. If the leaves have enough paint on them, encourage children to make more prints. Allow the prints to dry.

6. Hang the decorated mural paper on the bulletin board to brighten the classroom.

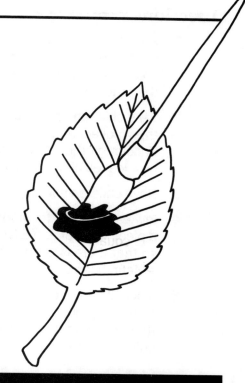

Pumpkins and Poetry

Children can create tissue-paper pumpkins and learn this short poem about what to do with a pumpkin.

Pumpkin, pumpkin on
   Halloween Day
Carved as a jack-o'-lantern,
To scare all away.
Pumpkin, pumpkin, we'll turn
   you into pie,
Eat pumpkin seeds, and then
   say good bye.

Materials

mural paper

orange construction paper

orange tissue paper

glue

scissors

marker

Directions

1. Cut a large pumpkin out of mural paper and on it write the above poem. Hang the cutout in the center of the bulletin board.

2. Cut smaller pumpkins out of orange construction paper.

3. Cut squares out of orange tissue paper.

4. Give children tissue-paper squares and glue. Have them crumple the tissue paper, dip it in the glue, and press it onto the pumpkin cutout.

5. When the tissue-paper pumpkins have dried, hang them around the poem.

How Many?

This geometric puzzle will keep children involved, counting how many triangles they can find. After the class has solved this puzzle you can encourage them to create their own geometry questions.

Materials

mural paper
construction paper
bulletin-board letters
marker

yarn
tape
tacks

Directions

1. Cover the bulletin board with mural paper.

2. Tape or tack the above yarn-triangle design on the bulletin board.

3. On the left side, hang up bulletin-board letters that read "How many triangles do you see?"

4. Fold a piece of construction paper in half. On the outside flap, write "The Answer." On the inside, write "47."

Jack-o'-Lantern

This bulletin board makes a wonderful learning center as well as a delightful room decoration. Children will enjoy finding new words within such a big word.

How many words can you make from these letters?

JACK-O'-LANTERN

can   real   near   cart   ear   cat   coal   jar   toe

Materials

mural paper	scissors
orange mural paper	markers
bulletin-board letters	chart paper

Directions

1. Cover bulletin board with mural paper (not orange).

2. Cut a large pumpkin shape out of orange mural paper. Using the markers, draw a jack-o'-lantern face on the cutout.

3. Hang the jack-o'-lantern in the center of the bulletin board and place the word JACK-O'-LANTERN above it.

4. Hang up bulletin-board letters to create the question, "How many words can you make from these letters?"

5. Distribute index cards or hang a piece of chart paper on the bulletin board on which children can record their answers.

How Did You Get to School Today?

Children learn about creating graphs and taking polls as they record how they traveled to school. The class may want to continue graphing other information about themselves, for example, hair color, favorite season, or bedtime.

Materials

mural paper	ruler	crayons
index cards	markers	glue

Directions

1. Hang the mural paper and, with a ruler, divide it into equal columns that represent possible modes of transportation children may use to get to school (walk, bike, car, bus, train).

2. With markers, draw simple pictures to illustrate each mode of transportation. Label each picture.

3. Distribute index cards and crayons to children and have them write their names on the cards.

4. Invite children to glue their cards in the column that shows how they got to school that day.

5. Tally up how many children use each mode of transportation. Which one do most children use?

I Am Afraid When . . .

You can extend the Halloween theme to include a way for children to express their feelings. Children can write or tell about what frightens them and perhaps begin to work through their fears.

Materials

mural paper

construction paper

writing paper

bulletin-board letters

pencils

scissors

stapler

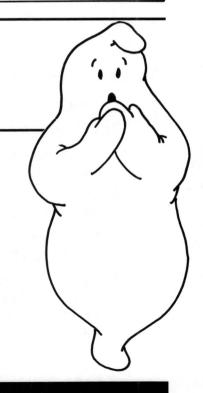

Directions

1. Cover the bulletin board with mural paper.

2. Discuss with children what it is like to feel afraid.

3. Distribute writing paper and pencils and ask children to write about what makes them feel afraid.

4. Trace and cut out from construction paper the pattern on page 93.

5. Staple children's essays and their Halloween cutouts in random order on the bulletin board.

6. Above their work, use bulletin-board letters to make a sign that reads "I Am Afraid When . . ."

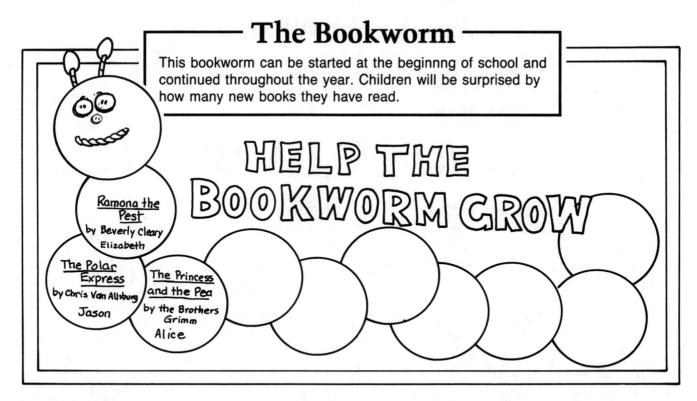

The Bookworm

This bookworm can be started at the beginnng of school and continued throughout the year. Children will be surprised by how many new books they have read.

HELP THE BOOKWORM GROW

Materials

mural paper	scissors
construction paper	stapler
bulletin-board letters	crayons
pipe cleaners	buttons

Directions

1. Hang the mural paper on the bulletin board.

2. Cut circles out of construction paper.

3. Using buttons for eyes and a nose, and pipe cleaners for a mouth and antennae, make a face on one circle.

4. Place the face on the bulletin board. Then staple the other circles in a row that winds around the perimeter.

5. In the center of the board, use bulletin-board letters to make a sign that reads "Help the Bookworm Grow."

6. Invite children to use crayons to fill in a circle of the worm every time they read a book. Tell them to write the name of the book, the name of the author, and their own name in the circle.

Seeds and More Seeds

Try this hands-on way of finding out about fruit seeds.
Children can cut open and remove the seeds from each fruit.
Then they can taste an assortment of different foods.

Materials

mural paper	knife	assorted fruit	scissors
white construction paper	ruler	(plum, apple, orange, watermelon)	glue
		markers	

Directions

1. Hang the mural paper on the bulletin board. Using a ruler, divide the bottom half into four horizontal rows.

2. At the beginning of each row, draw a picture of one of these fruits—plum, watermelon, apple, orange.

3. Invite children to watch as you cut open and seed each fruit. Save the fruit for children to taste later.

4. After the seeds are dry, have children glue the seeds in the appropriate row.

5. Cut speech balloons out of the white construction paper and write questions such as these inside each balloon: "Which fruit has the most seeds? Which fruit has the smallest seeds? Which fruit has only one seed?" Hang the balloons at the top of the bulletin board.

Numbers in Our World

Children may not realize how frequently we depend on numbers. This collage encourages children to think about how we use numbers in our lives.

Materials

mural paper

white construction paper

bulletin-board letters

crayons

scissors

glue

Directions

1. Cover the bulletin board with mural paper. At the top, use bulletin-board letters to create a sign that reads "We Use Numbers Every Day!"

2. Discuss with children the different places in which numbers are used on a daily basis.

3. Have children use construction paper and crayons to draw pictures that show how we use numbers.

4. Have children glue their pictures to the bulletin board.

Famous Scientists to Learn From

This bulletin board celebrates the importance of scientists in our lives.

Materials

mural paper	writing paper
bulletin-board letters	pencils or pens
book jackets	

Directions

1. Cover the bulletin board with mural paper. At the top, use bulletin-board letters to create a sign that reads "Read All About Them."

2. Beneath the sign display book jackets from biographies of various scientists.

3. Ask children to read a biography about a scientist they admire.

4. Distribute paper and pencils or pens for children to use to write book reports about the scientists. Display the book reports on the bulletin board.

How Many Pets Do You Have?

This bulletin board encourages children to compare the number of pets they have.

Materials

mural paper   markers
index cards   crayons
ruler   glue

Directions

1. Cover the bulletin board with mural paper. Use a ruler to divide it into equal columns that represent the different numbers of pets children have. Write the corresponding numbers in each column.

2. Distribute index cards and crayons and have children write their names and draw pictures of their pets on the cards. (Children who do not have pets may draw pictures of pets they would like to have.)

3. Invite children to glue their cards in the column that shows how many pets they have.

Illustrating Idioms

Children adore learning about idioms, and this bulletin board gives them a chance to illustrate the humor of idiomatic language and to interpret the idioms in their own way.

Materials

mural paper	markers	sentence-strip paper	crayons
construction paper	paint	stapler	tacks

Directions

1. Cover the bulletin board with mural paper.

2. Discuss idiomatic language with children. Help them to generate a list of familiar idiomatic phrases.

3. Distribute construction paper, paint, and crayons or markers to children. Have them illustrate an idiom.

4. Have children write the idioms they illustrate on pieces of sentence-strip paper (for speech bubbles).

5. Hang the mural paper on the bulletin board. Invite children to staple their finished pictures to the bulletin board.

6. Have children tack their sentence strips facedown under their pictures. They can take turns guessing the idioms that their classmates illustrated. Eventually, turn all the sentence strips to reveal the written idioms.

Rolled-Paper Turkey

As Thanksgiving approaches, help children to create a three-dimensional turkey bulletin board. Using paper and glue, the children can create a colorful new classroom friend.

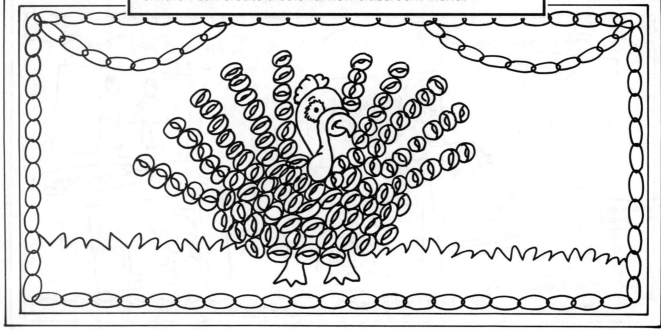

Materials

mural paper	pencils
construction paper	glue
tagboard	markers
stapler	scissors

Directions

1. Cover the bulletin board with mural paper.

2. Cut a large turkey shape out of tagboard and use markers to color in the head of the turkey.

3. Cut strips of construction paper.

4. Ask children to roll the strips around pencils to create tight rolls of paper.

5. Have children dip the rolls into glue and attach them to the tagboard turkey. Continue adding colored paper rolls until the body and tail of the turkey are covered with them.

6. When the glue has dried, staple the turkey to the bulletin board. It will be heavy, so use extra staples.

Our Storyland Friends

This bulletin board gives children a chance to write about and draw pictures of favorite characters from literature.

Materials

mural paper

bulletin-board letters

construction paper

stapler

crayons

white paper

scissors

Directions

1. Cover the bulletin board with mural paper.

2. Hold a discussion with children to find out who are their favorite characters from literature.

3. Distribute construction paper and scissors and have children cut out squares and triangles.

4. Tell children to make storyland houses by attaching squares of one color of paper to triangles of paper of a different color. Demonstrate if necessary.

5. Distribute white paper and crayons. Invite children to draw and color pictures of their favorite characters from literature and write several sentences about them.

6. Have them mount their pictures and sentences onto their houses and write the titles of the books and the characters' names on the roofs of their houses.

7. Staple the storyland houses to the bulletin board. Use bulletin-board letters to hang a sign that reads "Our Storyland Friends."

What Are We Thankful For?

Thanksgiving is a time to reflect about the good things in our lives. Children can make a class list about what they are thankful for and then illustrate their ideas.

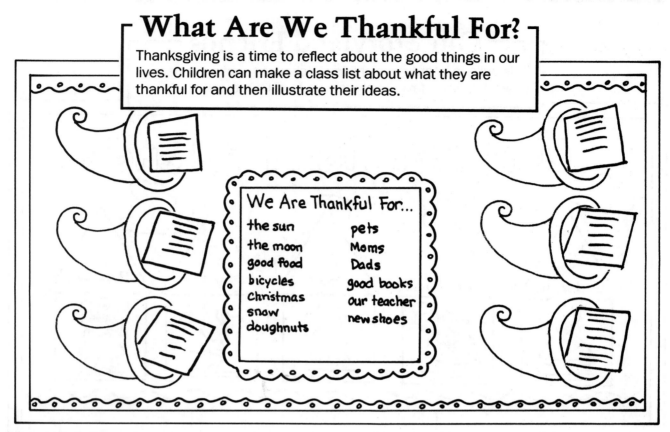

We Are Thankful For...

the sun   pets
the moon   Moms
good food   Dads
bicycles   good books
Christmas   our teacher
snow   new shoes
doughnuts

Materials

mural paper

brown and white construction paper

chart paper

markers

stapler

scissors

Directions

1. Cover the bulletin board with mural paper.

2. Discuss Thanksgiving and how we give thanks at this time of year. Make a class list of the many things to be thankful for. Record the children's ideas on chart paper.

3. Hang the chart paper in the center of the bulletin board.

4. Cut simple cornucopias (horns of plenty) out of brown construction paper. Attach white construction paper to the opening of each cornucopia.

5. Distribute markers and invite children to illustrate things they feel thankful for on the white paper inside the cornucopias. Some may write reports.

6. Have children staple their finished work on the bulletin board.

Odds and Evens

Symbols from the winter holidays help to create a seasonal bulletin board that teaches an important mathematics skill. Children practice recognizing odd and even numbers of bells, stars, dreidels, stockings, and candles.

Materials

mural paper

construction paper

bulletin-board letters

scissors

stapler

yarn

Directions

1. Hang the mural paper on the bulletin board.

2. Discuss odd and even numbers with children. Using concrete materials, have them practice deciding which groups have odd numbers of objects and which groups have even numbers.

3. At the top of the bulletin board, hang up bulletin-board letters that read "ODD" and "EVEN."

4. Trace and cut out the holiday patterns from page 93. Hang groups of each holiday symbol around the bulletin board. Some groups should have odd numbers of cutouts; others should have even numbers.

5. Invite children to string yarn from the word "EVEN" to the even-numbered groups of objects and from the word "ODD" to the odd-numbered groups of objects.

Where Do the Animals Live?

Learning about animals and their habitats helps children to understand how animals exist in nature. This cooperative mural gives children the opportunity to express their knowledge of how animals live.

ANIMAL HOMES

Materials

mural paper

paintbrushes

bulletin-board letters

paints

stapler

Directions

1. Discuss animal habitats with children.

2. Spread out mural paper on a flat surface and block off sections for different animals.

3. Distribute paints and brushes to children. Tell them to decide which animals will live in which sections and then to paint those sections accordingly.

4. After the mural dries, staple it to the bulletin board.

5. At the top of the bulletin board, use bulletin-board letters to make a sign that reads ''Animal Homes.''

6. Encourage children to write or dictate sentences about each animal and its home.

Which Dinosaur Is Which?

Learning about different dinosaurs is fun! This dinosaur bulletin board gives children a chance to match the dinosaurs to their names.

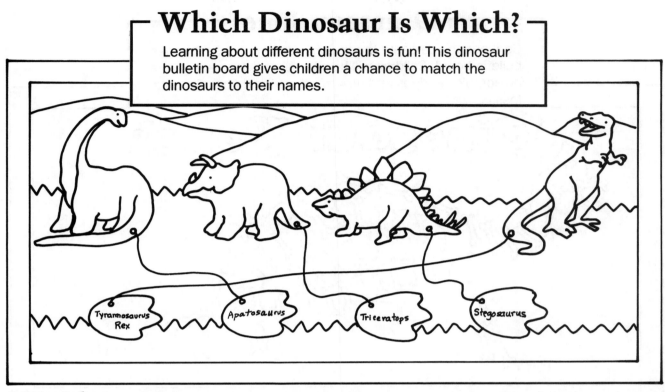

Materials

mural paper

sentence-strip paper

bulletin-board letters

yarn

dinosaur pictures

stapler

markers

tape

Directions

1. Cover the bulletin board with mural paper.

2. Discuss various dinosaurs with children.

3. Hang dinosaur pictures across the top of the bulletin board.

4. Write the name of each dinosaur on sentence-strip paper. Staple the paper strips to the bulletin board. The pictures and dinosaur names should be in scrambled order.

5. Staple a piece of yarn to each dinosaur picture. Attach a piece of tape to the loose end of the yarn. Encourage children to match the dinosaur pictures to the dinosaur names. You may need to replace the tape from time to time.

6. Use bulletin-board letters to create a sign that reads "Which Dinosaur Is Which?"

Dinosaur Bones

Continue the dinosaur theme by creating a dinosaur bones bulletin board. Children will be interested in learning what a paleontologist does and how much we learn from dinosaur fossils.

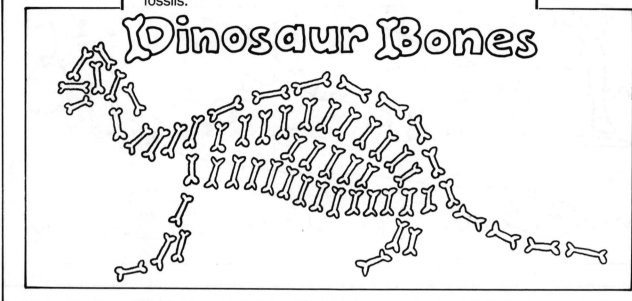

Materials

mural paper	tagboard	glue
clean, dried chicken bones	bulletin-board letters	stapler

Directions

1. Cover the bulletin board with mural paper.

2. Discuss dinosaur fossils and paleontology with children.

3. Collect or have children bring in clean, dried chicken bones.

4. Invite children to arrange the bones on tagboard to create dinosaur fossils.

5. Have children glue the fossils to the tagboard.

6. Staple the tagboard to the bulletin board for children to look at and discuss.

7. At the top of the bulletin board, use bulletin-board letters to create a sign that reads "Dinosaur Bones."

8. Add leftover bones to a sand table and encourage children to dig for dinosaur bones.

Paper-Strip Christmas Tree

This is a modern way to create an interesting and versatile Christmas tree. You can use the decorations described below or encourage children to bring in decorations from home.

Materials

mural paper   scissors

green construction paper   stapler

construction paper   glue

Directions

1. Hang the mural paper on the bulletin board.

2. Cut green construction paper into long strips. Glue several strips together to make the trunk of the tree. Staple that strip vertically onto the bulletin board.

3. Fasten the other green strips horizontally on the bulletin board across the trunk. The bottom strip should be the longest. Additional strips should become progressively shorter. When all the strips are attached, they should resemble a tree.

4. Encourage children to make paper decorations from construction paper. Have them cut out, color, and attach the decorations to the tree.

The Dreidel Song

These three-dimensional dreidels make wonderful holiday decorations. After children learn the words to "The Dreidel Song," they can learn to play the dreidel game. Rather than using money to play dreidels, try using goldfish-shaped or teddy bear-shaped crackers.

The Dreidel Song

I have a little dreidel,
I made it out of clay;
And when it's dry and ready,
Then dreidel I shall play.
Oh dreidel, dreidel, dreidel,
I made it out of clay;
Oh dreidel, dreidel, dreidel,
Now dreidel I shall play.

Materials

mural paper	hair spray	scissors
construction paper	stapler	chalk (not white)
chart paper		

Directions

1. Staple mural paper to the bulletin board.

2. Trace dreidel shapes on construction paper. Each child will need a pair of dreidel shapes.

3. Distribute the construction-paper tracings of dreidel shapes and scissors to children. Have them cut out the dreidel shapes.

4. Using the chalk, have children color designs on their dreidels. To prevent the chalk from smudging, spray hair spray on the children's finished designs.

5. Fold each dreidel in half vertically. Then staple the dreidels together at the edges so that altogether the open dreidel has four sides.

6. Write "The Dreidel Song" on chart paper. You may wish to cut the chart paper into the shape of a large dreidel.

7. Hang "The Dreidel Song" on the bulletin board and staple the dreidels around it. When you are ready to dismantle this bulletin board, children can attach string to the tops of their dreidels and hang them in their homes.

Holiday Character Puppets

This bulletin board is made from stick puppets the children construct themselves. Each puppet represents a character from a holiday story.

Which Holiday Story Is This Character From?

1.

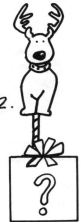
2.

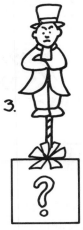
3.

4.

Materials

mural paper	crayons	writing paper
tagboard	scissors	glue
bulletin-board letters	stapler	markers
collage materials	craft sticks	

Directions

1. Cover the bulletin board with mural paper.

2. Read children holiday stories that have memorable characters. Then have each child choose a character to make as a stick puppet.

3. Set up the tagboard, glue, crayons, markers, scissors, and collage materials. Tell children to draw their puppet characters on tagboard and then to cut them out. Encourage children to embellish their puppets with collage materials.

4. When the puppets have dried, help children glue craft sticks to the backs of the cutouts to serve as handles.

5. Staple the puppets to the bulletin board and write a number beside each. In the bottom corner of the board, hang a piece of writing paper on which there is a corresponding numbered list that tells the name of each puppet.

6. Use bulletin-board letters to hang a sign that reads ''Which Holiday Story Is This Character From?'' Later, use the puppets in a skit.

Which Socks Match?

Making pairs of socks provides children with a fun and creative way to match designs.

Materials

mural paper
white construction paper
bulletin-board letters
stapler

paints
paintbrushes
scissors

Directions

1. Cover the bulletin board with mural paper. Hang bulletin-board letters that read "Which Socks Match?" at the top of the board.

2. Fold a piece of white construction paper in half. Trace the sock pattern from page 94 so that the long side of the sock is along the fold. Cut out the sock shape so that the folded side is still connected.

3. Give children sock shapes. Tell them to open the socks and, using paintbrushes, to drip different colors of paint on them. Tell children to fold the socks together and to press down on the backs of them. When children open the socks, they should look like mirror images of each other.

4. When the paint has dried, have children cut apart the socks. Collect the individual socks and mix them up. Invite children to match the socks that have the same designs.

5. You may want to hang the socks on the bulletin board in matching pairs or scatter them around so that children can play the matching game again.

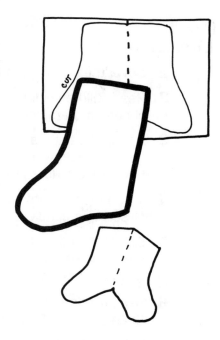

Patterns Around Us

These paper dolls provide an opportunity to discuss patterns in the environment. To make this activity more interesting, ask children to bring in fabric scraps.

Materials

mural paper   scissors
tagboard   glue
bulletin-board letters   crayons
fabric scraps

Directions

1. Cover the bulletin board with mural paper. Use bulletin-board letters to make a sign that reads "Patterns Around Us" and hang the sign on the bulletin board.

2. Distribute tagboard, crayons, and scissors. Have children draw the outline of a person on the tagboard and cut it out. The children may need some assistance, since tagboard is thick and difficult to cut.

3. Display various types of patterned fabric divided into groups that include stripes, flowers, checks, solid colors, dots, and so on. Discuss the various kinds of patterns with children. Tell them to choose a type of pattern and then to decorate their dolls with it by gluing the patterns to the outlines.

4. When the glue has dried, mount the dolls on the bulletin board. Children may want to name and label their dolls (for example—Dotty Dorothy or Stuart Striped Suit).

Our Senses

This bulletin board helps children learn about their senses and how they use them.

Materials

mural paper   scissors

old magazines   glue

pictures illustrating the senses   markers

Directions

1. Cover the bulletin board with mural paper.

2. Hang pictures of the five senses on the bulletin board and draw circles around each picture.

3. Distribute old magazines and scissors. Have children find and cut out pictures that show how each sense is used.

4. Help children draw a spoke from the circle around a particular sense. Then have them glue an appropriate picture at the end of the spoke.

5. You may wish to write the title ''Our Senses'' on the bulletin board.

My Name History

This bulletin board gives children a chance to explore the history behind their names and a way of discussing family backgrounds.

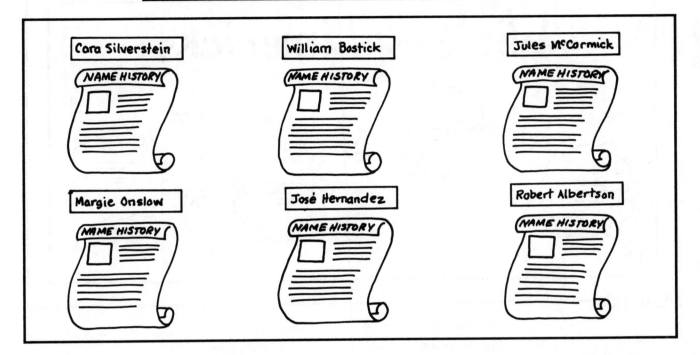

Materials

mural paper

sentence-strip paper

children's photographs

stapler

tape

white paper

Directions

1. Cover the bulletin board with mural paper.

2. Ask children to find out where their names come from and to record the information on white paper.

3. Have children bring in photographs of themselves and tape the pictures onto the white paper.

4. Write children's names on pieces of sentence-strip paper and hang them on the bulletin board.

5. Have children staple their information sheets and photographs underneath their names.

6. Use the information to discuss family backgrounds.

Wintery Limericks

This bulletin board gives children an exciting, seasonal way to display original limericks.

Materials

mural paper

bulletin-board letters

white construction paper

stapler

scissors

white lined paper

pencils or pens

Directions

1. Cover the bulletin board with mural paper.

2. At the top of the board, hang bulletin-board letters that read "Wintery Limericks."

3. Discuss limericks with children and read several to them. Then give them lined paper and pens or pencils with which to write their own limericks about winter.

4. Distribute white construction paper and scissors. Demonstrate how to make paper snowflakes by folding the paper several times and by cutting out small pieces. Have children make their own snowflakes. For six-sided snow-flakes, use round doilies.

5. Have children staple their snowflakes to the bulletin board. Encourage them to attach their poetry.

The Snowman

This three-dimensional snowman makes an interesting bulletin board as well as a fine cooperative project. Have children bring in Styrofoam packing peanuts.

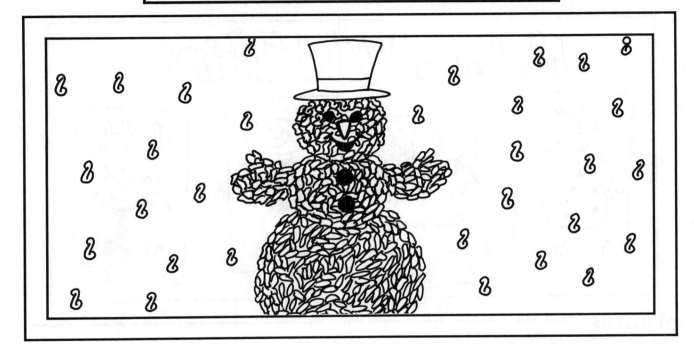

Materials

mural paper

white tagboard

Styrofoam packing peanuts

construction paper

stapler

glue

scissors

Directions

1. Cut the white tagboard into three circles of graduated sizes. They will be used to make the snowman.

2. Cut eyes, a nose, and a mouth out of construction paper.

3. Invite children to glue Styrofoam peanuts to the circles. Have one or two children glue the face onto the snowman.

4. Place the snowman on top of the mural paper and attach it with glue. Encourage children to glue extra peanuts around the snowman.

5. When the glue has dried, staple the completed snow scene to the bulletin board.

Make a Wild Thing

The classic story *Where the Wild Things Are* serves as inspiration for this bulletin board. Children have a chance to create their own "wild things."

Materials

mural paper	paintbrushes	scissors
cardboard	bulletin-board letters	paints
crayons	stapler	collage materials
construction paper	glue	

Directions

1. Cover the bulletin board with mural paper.

2. Set up the crayons, construction paper, cardboard, collage materials, glue, scissors, paints, and paintbrushes so that children can choose a medium.

3. After reading *Where the Wild Things Are* to children, discuss different imaginary monsters.

4. Invite children to create their own imaginary monsters using paints, collage materials, crayons, or a combination of the different media.

5. Staple the monsters to the bulletin board and, using bulletin-board letters, hang a sign that reads "Make a Wild Thing."

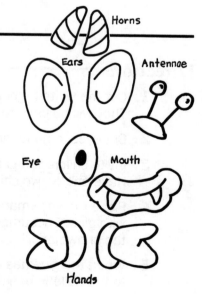

Mitten Weather

As children create matching mittens, they will learn about pairs and remember this poem about mitten weather.

Stripes or dots or sparkling white,
Mittens in winter fit just right.
Wool and cotton, maybe leather —
Mittens warm us in cold weather.
In rainbow colors and darkest black,
Mittens fit in a pocket or in your pack.
Thumbs alone, fingers together,
We love mittens in cold, cold weather.

Materials

chart paper   mural paper
markers   crayons
yarn   hole punch
construction paper

Directions

1. Cut a sheet of chart paper into the shape of a mitten and write the mitten poem on it.

2. Hang the poem in the center of a bulletin board that is covered with mural paper.

3. Have each child trace the pattern on page 94 onto two pieces of construction paper, then cut out the mittens.

4. Encourage children to color the mittens to form a pair.

5. Use a hole punch to make a hole at the top of each mitten.

6. Tie the mittens together with yarn and then hang them on the bulletin board.

Can You Name Each Quadrilateral?

This simple bulletin board is a fine way to begin discussing geometry. Children will quickly remember and use the names of the various quadrilaterals.

Materials

mural paper

stapler

bulletin-board letters

writing paper

construction paper

Directions

1. Cover the bulletin board with mural paper.

2. In the center of the bulletin board, hang bulletin-board letters to create a sign that reads ''Can You Name Each Quadrilateral?''

3. On the right side of the bulletin board, hang a piece of paper containing the names of different quadrilaterals. The list includes square, rectangle, rhombus, parallelogram, and trapezoid.

4. In the remaining space on the bulletin board, staple construction paper cutouts of each quadrilateral.

Printing Press

A Styrofoam meat tray with pencil markings makes a wonderful stamp. Children can display their stamps and their prints together on the bulletin board.

Materials

mural paper	paint rollers	paint
Styrofoam meat trays	rectangular shallow baking pans	pencils
white construction paper	stapler	tacks
		scissors

Directions

1. Staple mural paper to the bulletin board.

2. Cut the raised edges off the meat trays so that each tray is flat.

3. Distribute the meat trays and pencils with dull points. Ask children to draw pictures on the trays. Caution them not to pierce the trays.

4. Pour the paint into baking pans and set paint rollers and construction paper nearby. Have children dip the paint rollers into the paint and roll a thin layer of it onto their tray pictures.

5. Have children press the painted sides of the trays onto sheets of construction paper. When children lift the trays, beautiful prints will be visible.

6. When the paint dries, tack the trays and the prints to the bulletin board.

Famous African Americans

Recognizing the African Americans who contributed so much to our nation's history is a wonderful way to observe Black History Month.

Materials

mural paper

bulletin-board letters

photographs of famous African Americans

stapler

Directions

1. Cover the bulletin board with mural paper.

2. At the top of the bulletin board, hang bulletin-board letters to create a sign that reads "Famous African Americans."

3. Discuss notable African Americans such as Martin Luther King, Jr., Colin Powell, Thurgood Marshall, George Washington Carver, Harriet Tubman, Marian Anderson, and Jackie Robinson. Tell children to choose one of these people and to write a brief biography. Remind children to tell why they believe that person left a lasting mark in history.

4. Display pictures of these famous Americans on the bulletin board and below them staple corresponding biographies. Rotate the biographies so that each child has a chance to have his or her work displayed.

Naming Words and Doing Words

The terms "naming words" and "doing words" provide a gentle introduction to learning about nouns and verbs. Children will enjoy creating this bulletin-board list and can continue adding to it as they think of new words.

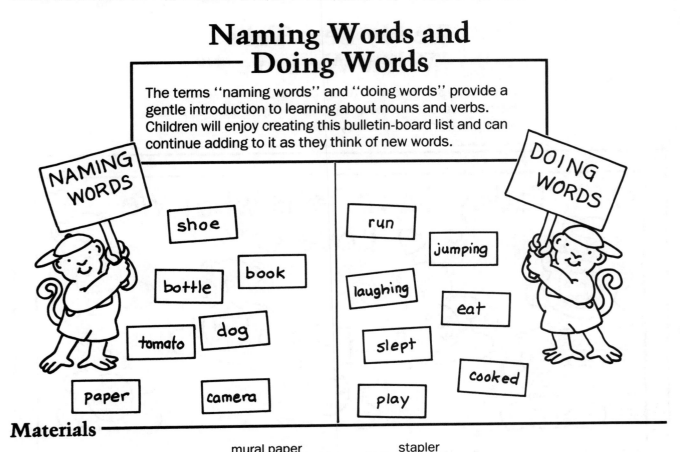

Materials

mural paper   stapler

construction paper   markers

sentence-strip paper   ruler

Directions

1. Cover the bulletin board with mural paper and draw a vertical line down the center using a marker and a ruler.

2. Use construction paper to make signs that read "Naming Words" and "Doing Words." Hang "Naming Words" at the top left side of the bulletin board; hang "Doing Words" at the top right side.

3. Write nouns and verbs on pieces of sentence-strip paper.

4. Discuss with children the difference between naming words and doing words. Give each child a sentence strip containing a word and have the child staple the strip to the appropriate side of the bulletin board.

5. Encourage children to think of other examples of doing words and naming words, to write them on sentence-strip paper, and then to add them to the bulletin board.

Teddy Bear Tells What We Love

All children seem to love teddy bears, and this seasonal bulletin board gives them an opportunity to express their feelings and create a cuddly friend.

Materials

mural paper

construction paper

crayons

stapler

scissors

Directions

1. Attach mural paper to the bulletin board.

2. Use the construction paper and the pattern on page 94 to trace and cut out a teddy bear for each child.

3. Have children discuss the things that they love.

4. Distribute teddy bear cutouts. Then ask children to use crayons to decorate their teddy bears. As the main decoration, tell children to write a list of the things they love on the teddy bears' bellies.

5. Staple the teddy bears to the bulletin board and add a sign that reads "Teddy Bear Tells What We Love."

We Remember the Presidents

Although it is Abraham Lincoln and George Washington who are honored especially on Presidents' Day, we can take this opportunity to learn about all the presidents of the U.S.

Materials

mural paper   writing paper

stapler   pens or pencils

Directions

1. Hang mural paper on the bulletin board.

2. Discuss the various presidents of the United States and have children choose a president to research. Tell children to write essays about each president's achievements and the problems he encountered during his presidency. Tell them also to find and bring in a picture of their chosen president.

3. Have children staple their essays and pictures on the bulletin board. Encourage them to report orally on the president they researched.

4. At the top of the bulletin board, hang a sign that reads "We Remember the Presidents."

Shadows and More Shadows

Making silhouettes helps children to understand that shadows are caused by objects intercepting rays of light. This bulletin-board idea is one way to start a discussion about shadows.

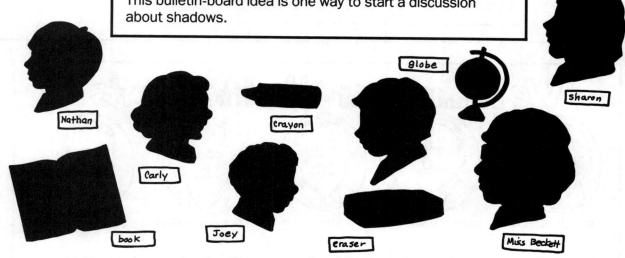

Materials

mural paper	scissors	markers
construction paper	stapler	tape
chair lamp without a shade	pencils	

Directions

1. Cover the bulletin board with mural paper.

2. Place a chair sideways a few inches (cm) away from a wall.

3. About ten feet (3 m) away from the wall, place a lamp without a shade.

4. Tape a piece of construction paper to the wall so that it is at the same level as a child's head would be when he or she is seated in the chair.

5. Tell a child to sit in the chair, then turn on the lamp.

6. Have another child trace a line around the shadow on the construction paper. In addition to making silhouettes of their heads, invite children to make silhouettes of classroom objects.

7. Cut out the silhouettes and staple them to the bulletin board. You may wish to have children label each silhouette.

8. Use a heavy marker to create a bulletin-board sign that reads "Shadows and More Shadows."

Fix the Broken Hearts

As children learn about short- and long-vowel sounds, they also begin to see word patterns. This seasonal bulletin board gives children a chance to practice their skills in a way that is creative and fun.

Materials

mural paper	scissors
red construction paper	stapler
bulletin-board letters	markers

Directions

1. Hang mural paper on the bulletin board.

2. Cut hearts out of red construction paper. Then cut each heart into two sections. The left section should be larger than the right section.

3. On the left piece of each heart, write a short-vowel word with a consonant-vowel-consonant pattern. On the right piece of each heart, write the letter e. Use words such as *mat-e, can-e, tap-e, hid-e, tub-e, not-e, cap-e, kit-e, rid-e, rip-e, cub-e,* and so on.

4. Staple the hearts to the bulletin board so that the left and right sides are slightly separated.

5. Use bulletin-board letters to create a sign that reads "Fix the Broken Hearts."

6. Ask children to read the words first as short-vowel words and then as long-vowel words. Encourage them to think of new words and have them create their own "broken hearts."

Can You Find the Perimeter?

Learning how to calculate perimeters is an important skill that takes practice. This bulletin board invites children to figure out the perimeters of actual objects.

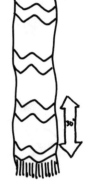
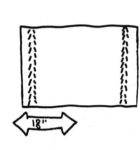

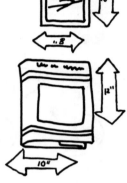

Materials

mural paper

construction paper

bulletin-board letters

square, rectangular, and triangular objects such as pennant, scarf, dish towel, book cover, photograph

stapler

markers

scissors

Directions

1. Cover the bulletin board with mural paper.

2. At the top of the bulletin board, use bulletin-board letters to make a sign that reads "Can You Find the Perimeter?"

3. Show children how to calculate the perimeters of squares, rectangles, and triangles. Let them practice calculating perimeters of assorted classroom objects.

4. Staple several square, rectangular, and triangular objects to the bulletin board.

5. Cut strips of construction paper so that each end has an arrow on it. Staple a paper strip beside the length and width of the square and rectangular objects. Write the size of each side on the paper strips. Repeat this process for the triangular objects.

6. Encourage children to figure out the perimeter of each object. You may want to change the objects from time to time so children can practice calculating perimeters of many different objects.

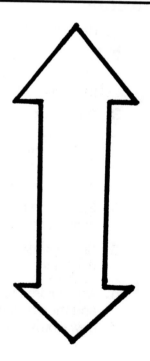

Pollution Solutions

This bulletin board gives children the opportunity to write and illustrate their ideas for solving the problem of pollution.

Materials

mural paper   stapler

bulletin-board letters   markers

pens or pencils   writing paper

Directions

1. Cover the bulletin board with mural paper.

2. At the top of the bulletin board, attach bulletin-board letters to make a sign that reads "Pollution Solutions."

3. Have children read about and discuss the different types of pollution (air, land, water) and what people can do to prevent pollution.

4. Invite each child to write an essay about one type of pollution. The essay should include suggestions for preventing the problem.

5. Staple the essays to the bulletin board.

6. Have children use markers to illustrate their ideas about ways of preventing pollution.

Recycling Works

Recycling is one way to cut down on waste products in the environment. This bulletin board helps children become aware of which products are recyclable and which are not.

Recyclable

THE NEWS

PAPER BAGS
CARDBOARD
ALUMINUM
GREETING CARDS
ENVELOPES
PLASTIC BOTTLES
GLASS
BOXES
OLD CLOTHES
USED SHOES
SHOPPING BAGS

Not Recyclable

MILK CARTONS
LIGHT BULBS
CELLOPHANE
CERAMICS
CANDY WRAPPERS
DISPOSABLE
   DIAPERS
DISPOSABLE
   RAZORS
WINDOW GLASS
TOOTHPASTE
   TUBES

Materials

mural paper	glue
old magazines	markers
scissors	ruler

Directions

1. Use a heavy marker and a ruler to draw a vertical line down the center of a large piece of mural paper.

2. On the left side, write the heading "RECYCLABLE"; on the right side, write "NOT RECYCLABLE."

3. Discuss with children how recycling helps the environment.

4. Help children compile a list of products that can be recycled and a list of ones that cannot be recycled. Write these products under the appropriate heading. Recyclable products include aluminum soda cans, newspapers, cardboard boxes, and greeting cards; nonrecyclable products include milk and juice cartons, disposable diapers, aerosol cans, lightbulbs, and ceramic objects.

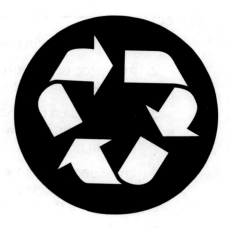

5. Encourage children to cut out magazine pictures of the various products and glue them on the mural paper.

6. Hang the mural paper on the bulletin board.

What's at the End of Your Rainbow?

This bulletin board offers children a chance to express their hopes, dreams, and wishes. Children also learn the different colors of the spectrum as they paint the colorful rainbow.

Materials

mural paper   stapler

paints   paintbrushes

yellow construction paper   scissors

glue

Directions

1. Set up paints, brushes, and mural paper on a large art table or on the floor.

2. Discuss the colors of the rainbow and the order in which the colors are arranged.

3. Have children paint a large rainbow on the mural paper.

4. Use the construction paper and the pattern on page 95 to trace and cut out a pot for each child.

5. Ask children to think about what they wish for. Have them write their names and wishes in their pots of gold.

6. Staple the mural paper with the rainbow in the center of the bulletin board. Glue the pots around the rainbow.

Potato-Print Shamrocks

Shamrock potato prints are a wonderful way to celebrate St. Patrick's Day.

Materials

mural paper

paints

green construction paper

potatoes

stapler

a knife

scissors

Directions

1. Cover the bulletin board with mural paper.

2. Cut several potatoes in half. Carve shamrock shapes out of the flat parts of the potatoes.

3. Cut shamrocks out of green construction paper and distribute them to children.

4. Set up paints and place potatoes nearby. Show children how to dip the potato into the paint, scrape off the excess paint, and press the potato onto the construction-paper shamrock to create a print.

5. Invite children to make potato-print shamrocks.

6. Staple the shamrock prints to the bulletin board.

Folk Tales from Around the World

This bulletin board brings together characters from folk tales from different parts of the world.

Materials

mural paper   stapler
crayons   scissors
construction paper

Directions

1. Cover the bulletin board with mural paper.

2. After reading and discussing an assortment of folk tales with children, ask them to select a favorite character.

3. Tell children to draw the character on construction paper and then to cut out their drawings.

4. Staple the characters to the bulletin board. Beneath each character, have each child make a label that tells the name of the character, the title of the story, and the country in which the story originated.

Stay Away!

This bulletin board will help to alert children to the dangers of substance abuse and provide springboards to lively discussion on this important subject.

Materials

mural paper	stapler
writing paper	pencils

Directions

1. Cover the bulletin board with mural paper.

2. Discuss substance abuse with children.

3. Tell children to find and clip newspaper and magazine articles about substance abuse and to bring those articles to class.

4. Invite children to write essays that express their own feelings about drug and alcohol abuse.

5. Staple the articles and essays in an interesting arrangement on the bulletin board.

6. At the top of the bulletin board, hang a sign that reads "Stay Away!"

What Time Is It?

Learning to tell time is an important life skill. This bulletin board gives children a hands-on way to use the clock.

Materials

mural paper

tagboard

white construction paper

brass fasteners

stapler

scissors

markers

Directions

1. Cover the bulletin board with mural paper.

2. Cut a large circle out of tagboard and draw a clockface on it.

3. Cut a minute and hour hand out of tagboard and attach them to the center of the clock with a brass fastener.

4. Staple the completed clock to the bulletin board.

5. Hold a discussion with children about the various times of day they do certain activities at home and at school.

6. Give children construction paper and markers and ask them to draw pictures of some of their daily activities. Tell them to label each picture with the appropriate time.

7. Hang the pictures around the clock. Encourage children to show the various times on the clock by moving the hands to the appropriate positions.

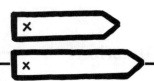

Healthy Eating

Nutrition is an important subject for children, and this bulletin board gives them the opportunity to explore the four food groups and what foods belong in each group.

Materials

mural paper   bulletin-board letters   glue

old magazines   stapler   ruler

markers   scissors

Directions

1. Use a ruler and marker to divide mural paper into four sections.

2. At the top of each section write the name of a food group—Milk and Cheese Products; Breads, Grains, and Pastas; Fruits and Vegetables; Meat, Fish, and Other Proteins.

3. Discuss the four food groups with children. Then ask them to look through old magazines to find pictures of foods in each group.

4. Have children cut out the pictures of the foods and glue them in the appropriate section on the mural paper.

5. When the glue dries, staple the mural to the bulletin board.

6. Use bulletin-board letters to create a sign that reads "Healthy Eating."

Weather Chart

Creating a weather chart is a fine way to learn about seasonal changes. Children can notice and record the different weather each day.

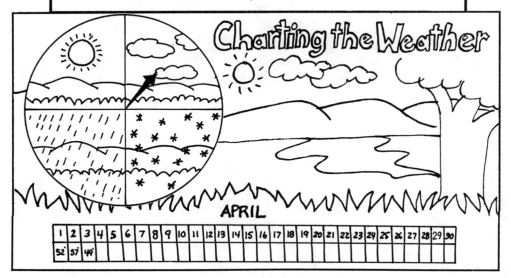

Materials

mural paper

markers

brass fastener

pictures of weather—
   (sunny, cloudy, rainy, snowy)

tagboard

crayons

scissors

stapler

ruler

Directions

1. Cover the bulletin board with mural paper.

2. Cut a large circle out of tagboard and divide it into quarters. Staple pictures that show the following four weather conditions: sunny, cloudy, rainy, snowy.

3. Cut an arrow out of the tagboard and attach it to the center of the weather wheel using the brass paper fastener. Mount the completed weather wheel on the left side of the bulletin board.

4. Divide a piece of tagboard into thirty columns and number the columns 1 to 30. With ruler and marker draw a horizontal line to divide the chart in half.

5. Hang the chart on the right side of the bulletin board beneath the heading "April."

6. Above the bulletin board, hang a sign that reads "Charting the Weather."

7. Each day have a different child set the weather wheel to the correct weather condition and record the day's weather by noting with crayon the weather condition for the corresponding day of the month. If you hang a thermometer outside of the classroom, this child can also record the daily temperature.

Circus Rhymes

This "Big Top" bulletin board is one way to reinforce rhyming words through the use of circus characters.

Materials

mural paper

pictures from circus programs

construction paper

white paper strips

stapler

markers

scissors

Directions

1. Cover the bulletin board with mural paper.

2. Cut a circus-tent border out of another piece of mural paper and color it with markers so that the "Big Top" has circus stripes. Staple the tent to the top of the bulletin board.

3. Draw and cut out from construction paper, or cut out from a circus program, pairs of pictures that are related to the circus. These pictures should include circus performers (jugglers, clowns, acrobats) and animals (elephants, dogs, lions, tigers).

4. Write pairs of rhyming words on paper strips and attach them to the pairs of circus performers and animals.

5. Attach the pairs of circus performers and animals to the bulletin board in a random fashion.

6. Encourage children to find the rhyming pairs under the "Big Top."

Compound Cookies

This giant cookie jar provides a fun way to practice compound words. Outside the jar are broken cookies that show the two parts of compound words. Inside the jar are completed cookie compound words. Children will enjoy creating their own cookies to add to this bulletin board.

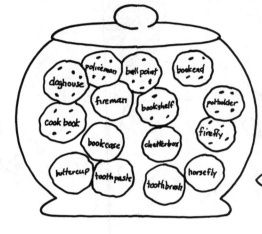

Materials

mural paper of two contrasting colors   markers

construction paper   stapler

scissors

Directions

1. Cover the bulletin board with mural paper of one color.

2. Cut a large cookie jar out of mural paper of a contrasting color. The cookie jar should fill a good portion of the board.

3. Discuss compound words with children. You may wish to generate a list of compound words with the class.

4. Have children cut "cookies" out of construction paper.

5. Invite children to write compound words on the cookies. Then tell them to cut some of the cookies between the two parts of the compound to make "broken" cookies.

6. Staple the "cookies" to the bulletin board. Place the whole cookies inside the cookie jar and the broken cookies around the outside. The broken pieces should be spaced slightly apart so that each word can be read separately or as one compound word. Children can continue adding "compound cookies" to the bulletin board as they think of new compound words.

7. Hang a sign above the bulletin board that reads "Compound Cookies."

Let's Fly a Kite

Colorful spring kites help to brighten a classroom and welcome the fine spring weather.

Materials

mural paper	scissors	white paper
paintbrushes	tissue paper	water containers
yarn	stapler	water

Directions

1. Staple mural paper to the bulletin board.

2. Cut kite shapes out of the white paper and cut the tissue paper into small, irregular shapes.

3. Distribute to each child the tissue paper, white kites, paintbrushes, and water containers.

4. Have each child place the tissue paper on the kite and paint over it with water. The colors of the tissue paper will run. After the tissue paper dries, it will fall off the kite and only the color will remain.

5. To make the tail, have children staple a piece of yarn to the kite. Then have them staple crumpled pieces of tissue paper to the yarn.

6. Have children staple their finished kites onto the bulletin board.

Crushed Easter Eggs

Children will enjoy this Easter egg bulletin board made from eggs! A few days before making this bulletin board, bring in, or have children bring in, crushed eggshells from home. The eggshells may be either white or brown.

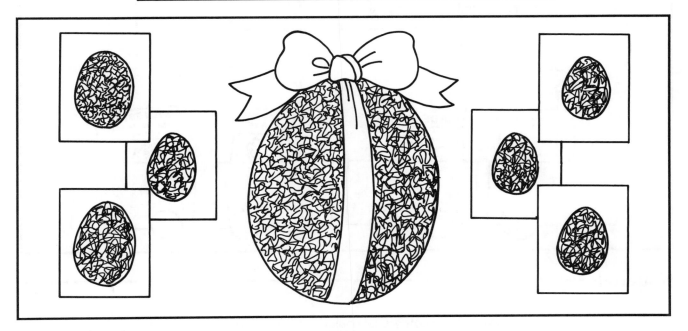

Materials

mural paper	glue
paintbrushes	paint
tagboard	crushed eggshells
scissors	stapler

Directions

1. Staple mural paper to the bulletin board.

2. Cut one large egg shape and smaller egg shapes out of tagboard.

3. Distribute paint, brushes, and tagboard eggs to children and have them paint the eggs. Let the painted eggs dry.

4. Distribute crushed eggshells to children. Have them spread glue on the painted eggs. Then ask them to sprinkle the eggshells over the glue.

5. When the glue dries, mount the textured Easter eggs on the bulletin board.

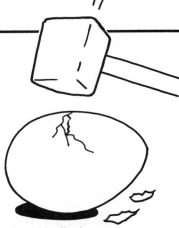

hard-boiled egg

Caldecott Train

The Caldecott Medal, awarded annually to the artist of the most distinguished picture book published in the United States, is named in honor of the English illustrator Randolph Caldecott. This bulletin board lets children create a train carrying their favorite characters from Caldecott Medal—winning books.

Materials

mural paper

Caldecott Medal books

construction paper

white paper

stapler

markers

scissors

crayons

Directions

1. Cover the bulletin board with mural paper.

2. Make a train from construction paper by cutting rectangles for the cars of the train and circles for the wheels. Staple the wheels to the cars and attach the train to the bulletin board.

3. Read several Caldecott Medal—winning books to children and have them tell which books they like best and which characters they find most appealing.

4. Distribute white paper, crayons, markers, and scissors. Invite children to draw and cut out book covers or pictures of their favorite characters.

5. Help children fit their characters into the train. Hang a sign at the top of the bulletin board that reads "Caldecott Train."

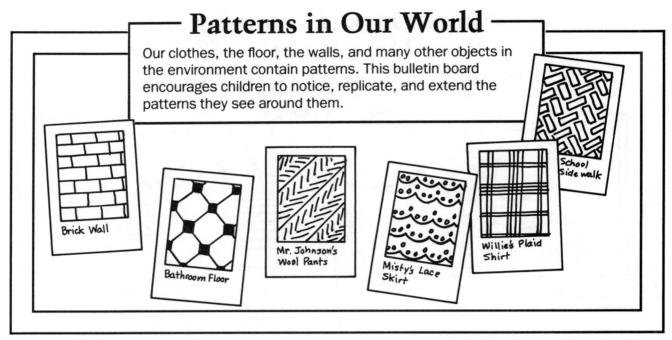

Patterns in Our World

Our clothes, the floor, the walls, and many other objects in the environment contain patterns. This bulletin board encourages children to notice, replicate, and extend the patterns they see around them.

Brick Wall

Bathroom Floor

Mr. Johnson's Wool Pants

Misty's Lace Skirt

Willie's Plaid Shirt

School Side walk

Materials

mural paper

white drawing paper

white construction paper

bulletin-board letters

stapler

crayons or pencils

Directions

1. Staple mural paper to the bulletin board.

2. Give students drawing paper and crayons or pencils. Then take them for a walk around the school or the neighborhood. Ask them to notice and sketch patterns they find interesting.

3. Upon returning to the classroom, distribute construction paper. Have children make careful replications of the patterns they sketched earlier.

4. Invite children to staple their patterns to the bulletin board along with labels telling where they saw the patterns. Older children may wish to write a few sentences telling why they found the pattern interesting.

5. Use bulletin-board letters to create a sign that reads "Patterns in Our World."

6. Encourage children to add patterns from different locations, such as their homes, the park, the grocery store, and so on. They can also create patterns of their own to staple to the bulletin board.

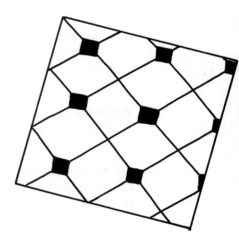

Where Does It Come From?
How Does It Get to Us?

This bulletin board is a good way to collect information about where different fruits and vegetables come from and how they reach us.

Materials

mural paper	bulletin-board letters	scissors
construction paper	stapler	glue
writing paper	crayons or markers	
old magazines	pencils	

Directions

1. Staple mural paper to the bulletin board with a bulletin-board letter sign above it that reads "Where Does It Come From? How Does It Get to Us?"

2. Hold a discussion about different fruits and vegetables. Distribute writing paper and pencils. Have children form small groups and decide which fruit or vegetable they would like to research and write about. Tell children that they should make notes on information such as where and how their fruit or vegetable grows, what products are made from it, and how it gets from where it is grown to the store or market where it is sold. Ask children to tell you what fruits or vegetables they will research. Make sure no two groups are researching the same ones.

3. While they are researching and writing, cut out magazine pictures of the fruits and vegetables children have selected and hang the pictures across the top of the bulletin board.

4. Cut enough arrows from construction paper so that pictures at the top will have three arrows pointing down from them. Glue the arrows on the bulletin board beneath the pictures.

5. For each picture, beneath the left arrow, hang the group's paragraph about where and how the food grows. Beneath the center arrow, hang the paragraph about what products are made from the food. Beneath the right arrow, hang the paragraph that tells how the food gets to the store or market. Allow children to illustrate their paragraph using crayons or markers.

Neighborhood Maps

This bulletin board gives children the opportunity to use map skills in a practical way.

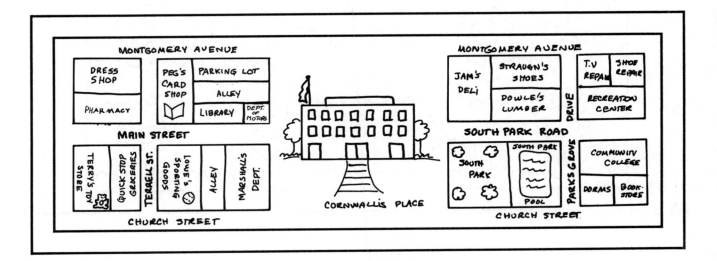

Materials

mural paper	maps	markers
yardsticks/metersticks	rulers	crayons
pencils	stapler	

Directions

1. Show children different kinds of maps and discuss their purposes. Explain to children that they will be creating a map of the school neighborhood.

2. Under your supervision, have groups of children use measuring tools to measure the distance from the school to the ends of one or two nearby streets. Ask them to note the buildings, signs, and other neighborhood sights they see.

3. Back in the classroom, have each group of children report on the information they gathered. Help them decide on a scale for the map.

4. Spread the mural paper on a table or on the floor. Invite several children to create a pencil sketch of the school and neighboring streets. Help them to make sure that the sketch is drawn to scale.

5. Encourage the rest of the class to use crayons to color in the various streets, intersections, buildings, signs, and other landmarks on the map.

6. Have children use markers to label the streets.

7. Staple the finished map to the bulletin board.

Homophone Garden

Homophones are words that are pronounced the same but have different meanings and different spellings. This seasonal bulletin board helps children learn different homophones.

Materials

mural paper   stapler

construction paper   scissors

markers

Directions

1. Staple mural paper to the bulletin board.

2. Distribute construction paper, scissors, and markers to children. Have them fold the paper in half.

3. Demonstrate how to draw a flower on the folded paper so that when they cut out the drawing they will have two identical flowers. Allow children to make flowers.

4. Discuss what homophones are and have children generate a list of homophones.

5. Invite children to write one word of a homophone pair on one of their flowers. Tell them to write the other word of the pair on the other flower.

6. Hang the flowers on the bulletin board so that the matching pairs are not next to each other.

7. At the top of the bulletin board, write a sign that reads "Homophone Garden."

8. Encourage children to find the pairs of flowers by matching homophones. Have children continue adding flowers to the bulletin board as they think of new homophones.

Tissue-Paper Flowers

Folding tissue paper to make flowers is a novel and exciting way for children to decorate a bulletin board.

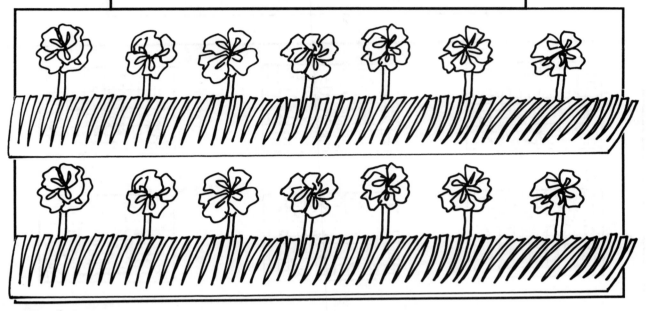

Materials

mural paper   tissue paper

green construction paper   stapler

scissors   tape

Directions

1. Staple mural paper to the bulletin board.

2. Distribute tissue paper, scissors, and tape. Show children how to make accordion folds. Place three pieces of tissue paper on top of one another. Then make 1-inch (2 1/2-cm) folds in alternating directions until the tissue paper is like an accordion or a fan. Put a piece of tape around the center of the folded tissue paper and then trim the edges to round them out.

3. Show children how to lift each piece of tissue paper carefully to create a flower.

4. Help children staple their flowers to the bulletin board.

5. Distribute green construction paper. Invite children to cut paper strips for stems and to staple the stems under the flowers. Have children cut paper fringes for grass and attach them to the bottom of the bulletin board.

Personal Flags

As Flag Day approaches, children will enjoy creating their own personal flags.

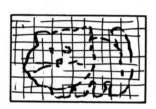  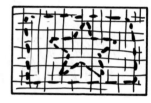

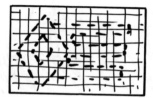  

Materials

mural paper

porous fabric (burlap, muslin)

darning needles

white paper

stapler

yarn

markers

scissors

pins

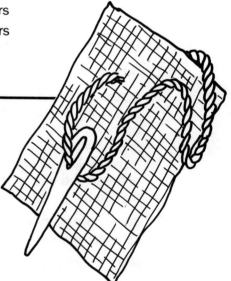

Directions

1. Staple mural paper to the bulletin board.

2. Distribute white paper, scissors, and markers. Tell children to create a special design for their own flag. Have them draw an outline of the design on the white paper and then cut it out.

3. Give children fabric and pins. Have them pin their designs to the fabric and draw the outline on the fabric.

4. Invite children to stitch their design onto their flag, using yarn and the darning needles.

5. Display the finished flags on the bulletin board. Children may wish to write short descriptions explaining their designs.

Newbery Medal Winners

The Newbery Medal was named for British publisher John Newbery, who is widely considered to be the father of children's literature because he was the first person to publish books specifically for children. This bulletin board gives children a place to express their reactions to Newbery Medal-winning books.

Materials

mural paper   stapler

white construction paper   markers

writing paper   scissors

pencils

Directions

1. Staple mural paper to the bulletin board.

2. Discuss Newbery Medal-winning books with children and have each child choose a book to read.

3. After allowing time for children to finish their books, distribute writing paper and pencils. Ask children to write about the books they read. Have them tell if they think the books deserved the award, and why.

4. Distribute white construction paper, scissors, and markers to children. Tell them to make fancy signs containing the title of the book they read.

5. Mount children's signs and reviews on the bulletin board.

6. Hang a sign above the bulletin board that reads "Newbery Medal Winners."

What Fraction of Each Shape Is Shaded?

This bulletin board challenges children to work with fractions.

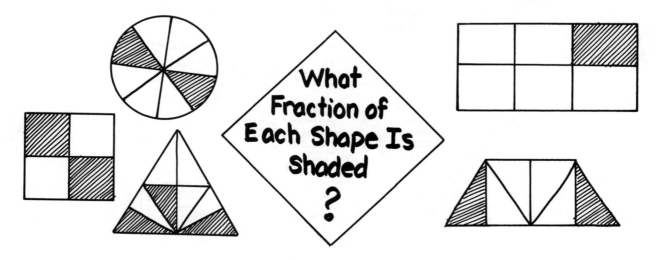

Materials

mural paper

white construction paper

bulletin-board letters

ruler

stapler

markers

scissors

Directions

1. Staple mural paper to the bulletin board.

2. Using bulletin-board letters, hang in the center of the bulletin board a sign that reads "What Fraction of Each Shape Is Shaded?"

3. Using a ruler and markers, draw several geometric shapes on white construction paper. Divide each shape into equal sections and shade as many sections as you choose. Cut out the shapes and attach them to the bulletin board.

4. Invite children to use fractional terms, such as 3/8, 1/6, 2/8, to decide what part of each shape is shaded. Remind children to reduce their fractions where appropriate.

5. You may wish to have children create their own shaded shapes to hang on the bulletin board so that others can identify the fractions represented.

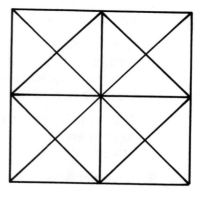

What Kind of Home Do You Live In?

Making this chart about different types of homes gives children a hands-on way of learning about graphs.

Dana
Bill
Cynthia
Althea

Betty
Harold
Joe

Vivian
Eliza
Gerald
Jason

Materials

mural paper   stapler

paper strips   marker

bulletin-board letters   ruler

crayons

Directions

1. Use a ruler and marker to divide a piece of mural paper into enough columns to represent the different types of homes in which the children in your class live.

2. Discuss with children the different types of homes in which they live. Call on volunteers to make crayon drawings of these homes in the separate columns of the mural paper.

3. Distribute small paper strips to children. Tell them to write their names on the paper and then to staple the paper in the column that shows the type of home in which they live.

4. Staple the mural paper to the bulletin board.

5. Use bulletin-board letters to hang above the bulletin board a sign that reads ''What Kind of Home Do You Live In?''

6. Encourage children to tally the names in the columns. Have them tell which kind of home most of the children live in and which kind of home only a few children live in. Have children use their findings to make a class bar graph.

Unscramble the Zoo Animals' Names

Spring is a wonderful time for visiting the zoo and seeing the baby animals and various zoo exhibits. This bulletin board is an engaging animal mural, featuring scrambled animal names.

Materials

mural paper	scissors	markers
construction paper	glue	crayons
bulletin-board letters	stapler	tape

Directions

1. Discuss zoos and zoo animals with children. Help them to make a list of animals they might see at a zoo.

2. Set up a table with construction paper, scissors, tape, glue, crayons, and markers. Invite children to create paper versions of zoo animals and other things found in a zoo.

3. Place a large piece of mural paper on the floor. You may wish to draw a few lines designating specific areas of the zoo, such as the picnic area, the elephant house, the reptile house, the entrance, and so on. As children finish making their zoo animals and other objects, have them glue their work to the mural paper.

4. Encourage children who finish making their animals early to make paper grass or to color roads. These details will fill the empty spaces on the mural.

5. When the mural is complete and the glue has dried, staple it to the bulletin board.

6. At the top of the bulletin board, hang a bulletin-board-letter sign that reads "Unscramble the Zoo Animals' Names." Around the border of the mural, show scrambled names of the animals that are pictured in the mural, such as aesl (seal), tanelphe (elephant), grite (tiger), and so on.

Balloons and More Balloons

Nothing brightens up a classroom wall like balloons. This bulletin board will give children a chance to make colorful balloons of all shapes and sizes.

Materials

mural paper

construction-paper

trays of assorted paper scraps

yarn

stapler

glue

scissors

Directions

1. Cover the bulletin board with mural paper.

2. Cut large balloon shapes out of construction-paper.

3. Distribute the balloon shapes and glue to children. Set out trays that contain an assortment of paper scraps. You might use leftover wrapping paper, tissue-paper scraps, and construction-paper scraps.

4. Invite children to decorate their balloons using the paper scraps and glue.

5. When the glue dries, staple the balloons to the bulletin board and attach a piece of yarn to each one.

Fairy-Tale Theater

Creating a bulletin board of fairy tale stick puppets under a theater curtain is an excellent way to extend a unit on fairy tales.

Materials

mural paper

large pieces of fabric

craft sticks

scissors

fabric scraps

tagboard

glue

crayons

ribbon

stapler

yarn

buttons

Directions

1. Cover the bulletin board with mural paper.

2. Drape and staple along the top and sides of the bulletin board large pieces of fabric to form a theater curtain. You may wish to draw a stage at the bottom of the bulletin board.

3. Help children make a list of fairy-tale characters. Ask them each to choose one of the characters to make as a puppet.

4. Have children make the bodies of their puppets by gluing pieces of tagboard together and attaching craft sticks to the backs of the bodies.

5. Set out crayons, fabric scraps, ribbon, buttons, yarn, and any other collage materials you have. Invite children to embellish their characters using these materials.

6. When the glue on the puppets has dried, encourage children to put on puppet shows. These can be original stories or traditional fairy tales.

7. When all the performances are over, hang children's puppets on the bulletin board and encourage children to talk about each fairy tale.

Right and Left Animal Mural

Children can look at their favorite animals while recognizing the difference between left and right.

Materials

mural paper   glue

construction paper   ruler

bulletin-board letters   crayons

Directions

1. Hang the mural paper on the bulletin board and draw a line down the center of it to divide it in half.

2. At the top of the right-hand side, glue the bulletin-board letters ''right'' and an animal that is facing right. At the top of the left-hand side, glue the bulletin-board letters ''left'' and an animal that is facing left.

3. Invite children to use construction paper and crayons to draw their own animal pictures. Have them attach their pictures to the corresponding side of the chart.

Picture-Perfect Pets

A pet can be a very important part of a child's life. Pets teach children about responsibility, affection, and friendship. Even children who don't have pets enjoy the opportunity to think about animals in their neighborhood or a pet they dream about owning. This bulletin board lets children express their feelings about having a pet.

Materials

mural paper	stapler
white construction paper	crayons
photographs of pets	pencils

Directions

1. Staple mural paper to the bulletin board.

2. Discuss pet ownership with children. Have them tell about their own pets or about pets they would like to have.

3. Distribute construction paper, crayons, and pencils. Ask children to draw a picture of their pet and under it to write what they like best about their pet. Children who don't have pets can draw and write about a pet they would like to own.

4. Hang children's work on the bulletin board with a sign above it that reads "Picture-Perfect Pets." If children have a photograph of their pet, encourage them to bring it in to hang next to their work.

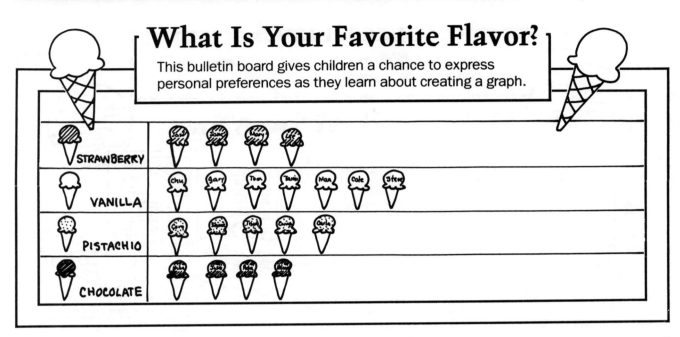

What Is Your Favorite Flavor?

This bulletin board gives children a chance to express personal preferences as they learn about creating a graph.

Materials

mural paper	scissors	crayons
bulletin-board letters	marker	ruler
construction paper	glue	stapler

Directions

1. Ask children to name their favorite ice-cream flavors.

2. Use a ruler and marker to divide mural paper into enough rows to represent the different flavors mentioned.

3. Cover the bulletin board with the mural paper.

4. Make ice-cream cones of the different flavors mentioned by cutting triangles and circles out of construction paper.

5. At the left side of each row on the mural paper, glue or staple a cone and write the name of the flavor.

6. Use bulletin-board letters to make a sign that reads ''What Is Your Favorite Flavor?''

7. Distribute cones to children and have them write their names on them. Be sure that each child gets a cone that represents his or her favorite flavor ice cream.

8. Invite children to attach their cones to the row that represents their favorite flavor.

9. Encourage children to count the cones in each row to see which flavors are the most and least popular.

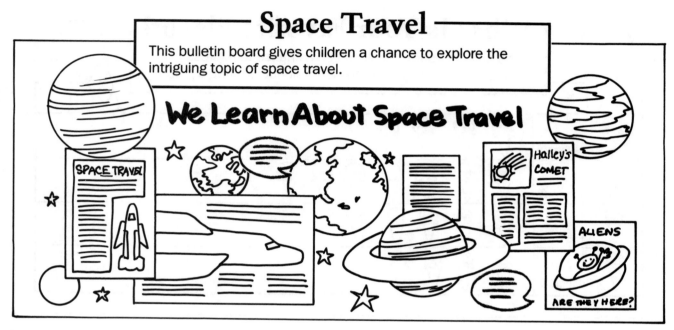

Materials

mural paper	newspaper articles	crayons
white paper	scissors	pencils
bulletin-board letters	stapler	photographs

Directions

1. Staple mural paper to the bulletin board.

2. Discuss space travel with children. Encourage them to read about various space missions, astronauts, the planets, the sun, the moon, the stars, and so on.

3. Have each child choose and research a topic. Some possible reference sources are current or old news articles about space travel, biographies of astronauts, encyclopedia articles or textbook chapters on stars.

4. Have children each write a paragraph summarizing what they learned about their topic. Tell them to illustrate their paragraphs. Have children write their paragraphs on white paper shaped like thought bubbles.

5. Encourage children to collect newspaper articles or photographs about space travel.

6. In the center of the bulletin board, use bulletin-board letters to make a sign that reads "We Learn About Space Travel." Then help children to make a montage of their paragraphs and the newspaper clippings and photographs.

Our Heritage

The United States is commonly thought of as a melting pot of different cultures and people from different lands. This bulletin board encourages children to find out about their ancestors and where they came from.

Materials

mural paper	writing paper	stapler
construction paper	pencils	crayons
photographs	scissors	tape
drawing paper		

Directions

1. Staple mural paper to the bulletin board.

2. Use construction paper and the pattern on page 95 to make a large map of the United States. Hang it on the bulletin board.

3. Discuss the notion of immigration with children. You may wish to read several books to the class about immigrant families or about why various groups of people left their homelands to build new lives in other countries.

4. Have each child find out and write a paragraph telling the country from which their family came, why they left their homeland, and on what basis they came to their new country. Encourage children to bring in old or new photographs of their families or to draw older members of their family, using drawing paper and pencils and/or crayons.

5. Invite children to tape their finished work around the map.

6. Hang a sign at the top of the bulletin board that reads "Our Heritage."

Fish Swim, Birds Fly

Children will delight in learning how to fold an ordinary piece of paper into a fish or a bird. Integrate these origami animals into a scenic bulletin board.

To make the origami fish or bird, begin with a square held as a diamond.

1. Fold bottom point up to top point to form triangle.

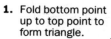

2. Fold point down until it touches the base.

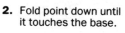

3. Fold side point inward to make the nose of the fish.

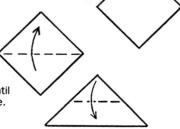

4. Fold back point up to make a fin.

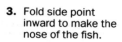

5. Turn the fish around and decorate it with eyes, mouth, gills and so on.

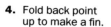

1. Fold bottom point up to top point to form triangle.

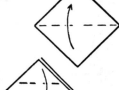

2. Fold point down until it touches the base.

3. Fold the top edge over the point a little.

4. Fold the point over the new fold.

5. Lift the bird and fold in half to form wings.

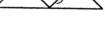

6. Fold and unfold the wings.

7. Fold and unfold the wings again in another spot.

8. Raise wings into flying position.

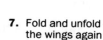

9. Decorate the bird.

Materials

mural paper   paintbrushes   stapler   construction paper

paints   scissors   crayons

Directions

1. Set out mural paper, paints, and paintbrushes.

2. Invite a group of children to paint an ocean on the mural paper to serve as a background. Let the mural paper dry and staple it to the bulletin board.

3. Discuss origami with children and show them how to make a bird and a fish (see instructions above). Encourage them to decorate their origami animals and hang them on the bulletin board, placing the fish in the water and the birds in the sky.

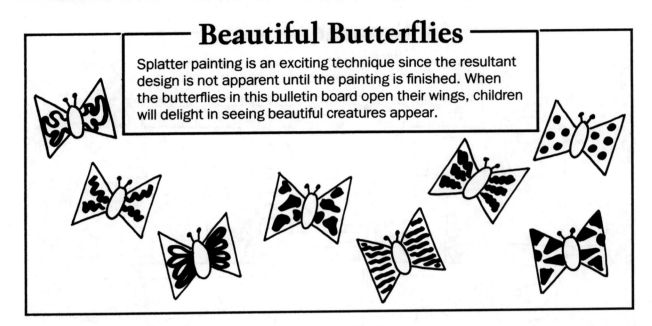

Beautiful Butterflies

Splatter painting is an exciting technique since the resultant design is not apparent until the painting is finished. When the butterflies in this bulletin board open their wings, children will delight in seeing beautiful creatures appear.

Materials

mural paper	stapler
white paper	paints
paintbrushes	pipe cleaners
scissors	tape

Directions

1. Hang mural paper on the bulletin board.

2. Distribute white paper and scissors and have children fold the paper in half. Show them how to cut out two triangles that are attached by the points.

3. Set out paints and paintbrushes. Invite children to splatter paint on the open triangles. Then have them fold the triangles together and press on the closed shape. After several seconds, have children open the triangles to see a symmetrical design.

4. Have children cut out from the remains of their white paper oval shapes for the bodies of their butterflies. Encourage them to paint the ovals.

5. Distribute pipe cleaners and have children attach them to the butterflies to serve as antennae.

6. When the splattered triangles are dry, have children tape the bodies to the wings to create butterflies.

7. Staple the butterflies to the bulletin board.

A Summer Picnic

Summer is a wonderful time to go on a picnic, and children will enjoy creating a bulletin board around this theme.

Materials

gingham tablecloth or mural paper

construction paper, brown and other colors

scissors

stapler

crayons

Directions

1. Cover the bulletin board with a gingham tablecloth or mural paper that looks like a picnic blanket.

2. Onto brown construction paper, trace the pattern of a picnic basket on page 96. Make sure you trace enough baskets so that each child gets one.

3. Discuss picnics with children. Have them list the various things they might pack in a picnic basket.

4. Distribute the traced picnic baskets and scissors. Have children cut out the baskets and decorate them on the outside.

5. Distribute construction paper and crayons. Ask children to draw, color, and cut out the foods they would like to take on a picnic.

6. When children have finished, invite them to staple their baskets to the bulletin board. Then have them staple their foods in or around the baskets. Soon the picnic blanket will be filled with a delicious and colorful meal!

The Man on the Moon?

The notion of "the man on the moon" is a quaint and time-honored one. The children's ideas on the topic can be entertaining as well as revealing.

Materials

dark mural paper	yarn and fabric scraps	crayons
white mural paper	scissors	paintbrushes
yellow paint	stapler	glue

Directions

1. Cover the bulletin board with dark mural paper.

2. Cut a large circle out of white mural paper and set it out on a large table.

3. Mix glue with yellow paint. Set out the paint/glue, brushes, yarn, and fabric scraps. Ask children to paint the entire surface of the circle and then to decorate it with the yarn and fabric. The yarn and fabric scraps will stick to the circle when it dries. Have children discuss what the face might look like and then invite one child to draw that face on the moon.

4. Staple the circle to the bulletin board.

5. Have children discuss the idea of "a man on the moon." Invite them to write or tell about how the man got there and why he stays.

Big, Bigger, Biggest

This bulletin board gives children the opportunity to compare objects by size.

Materials

mural paper

white construction paper

bulletin-board letters

stapler

crayons

scissors

Directions

1. Cover the bulletin board with mural paper.

2. Cut out from construction paper the following items in three different sizes: three stars, three pennants, three drums, three apples, three ice-cream cones.

3. Distribute the cutouts and ask children to decorate them using crayons.

4. Have children staple their finished work to the bulletin board. The items in a group need not be together.

5. Use bulletin-board letters to make a sign that reads "Big, Bigger, Biggest."

6. Invite children to find each set of like items. Have them compare the pictures using the words *big, bigger, biggest.*

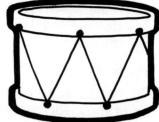

The Spider's Web

Folk tales from around the world are timeless and enchanting, and the stories about Anansi are especially so. Reading *Anansi the Spider* and creating this spider-web bulletin board make a wonderful introduction to folk tales from different parts of the world.

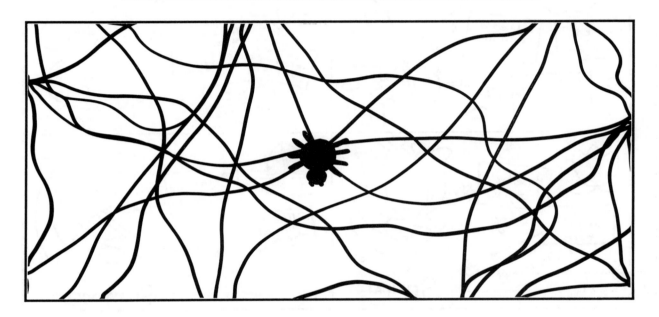

Materials

mural paper	stapler
black construction paper	yarn
tacks	tape
Anansi the Spider	scissors

Directions

1. Cover the bulletin board with mural paper.

2. After reading *Anansi the Spider* to children, discuss spider webs. Invite small groups of children to string yarn on the bulletin board in an assortment of directions. Attach the yarn to the bulletin board using tacks, staples, and tape.

3. Cut out from construction paper two circles and eight thin strips. Make a spider by overlapping the circles and attaching the strips. The circles form the body of the spider; the strips of paper form the legs.

4. Place the spider in its bulletin-board web.

The Four Seasons

This bulletin board is a way for children to express their thoughts and feelings about the seasons.

Materials

mural paper   stapler

markers   ruler

crayons

Directions

1. Cover the bulletin board with mural paper and, with a ruler and marker, divide the paper into quarters.

2. At the top of each section, draw a picture to represent the season and beneath it write the name of the season. For example, a snowman might represent winter; a flower, spring; a beach ball, summer; and a red, gold, or yellow leaf, fall.

3. Invite children to use crayons to write their thoughts about each season in the appropriate box.

4. After children finish writing, have them read their thoughts aloud.

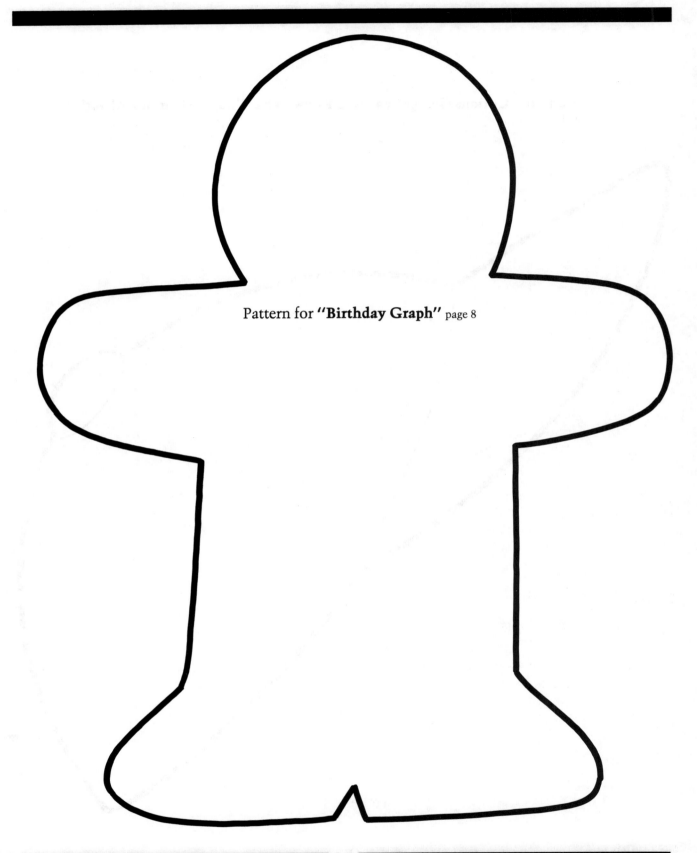

Pattern for **"Birthday Graph"** page 8

Pattern for **"Curious George Wants to Know What You Are Curious About"**
page 12

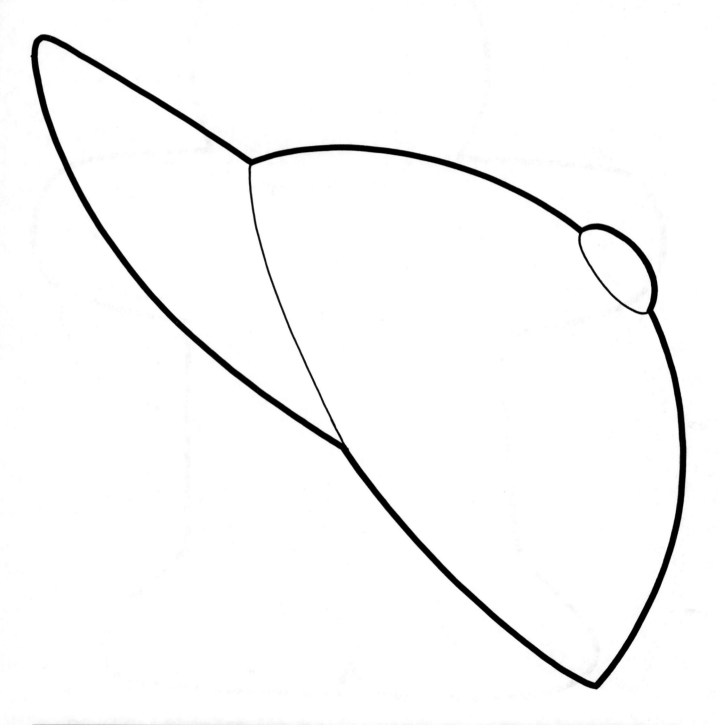

Pattern for **"I Am Afraid When"** page 19

Patterns for **"Odds and Evens"** page 29

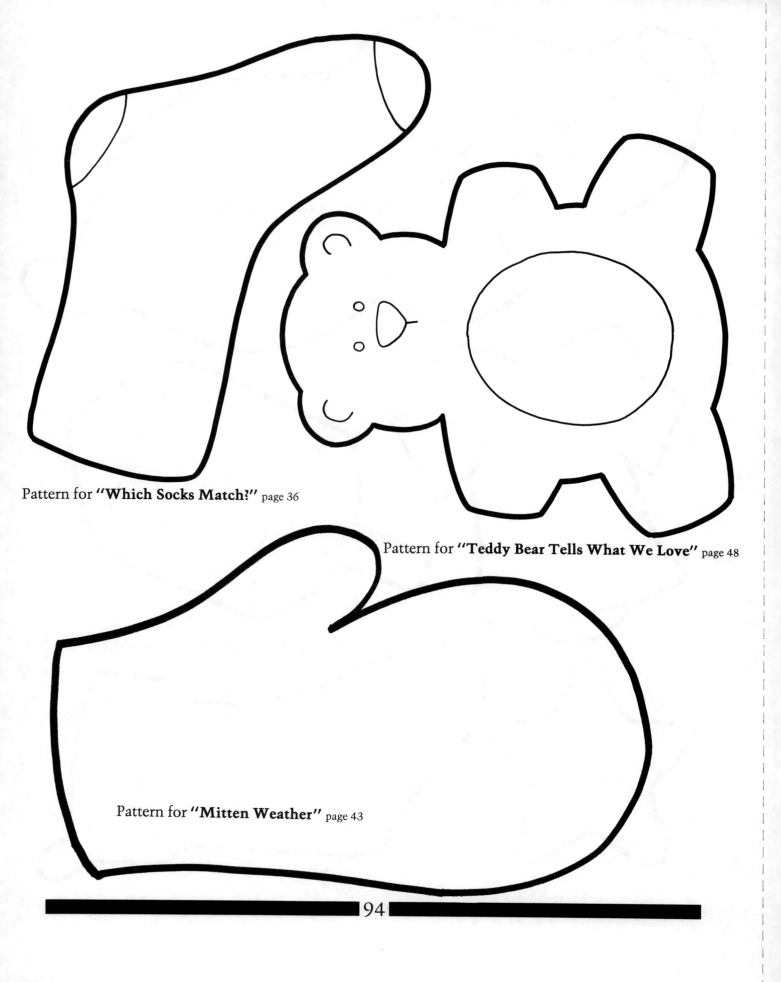

Pattern for **"Which Socks Match?"** page 36

Pattern for **"Teddy Bear Tells What We Love"** page 48

Pattern for **"Mitten Weather"** page 43

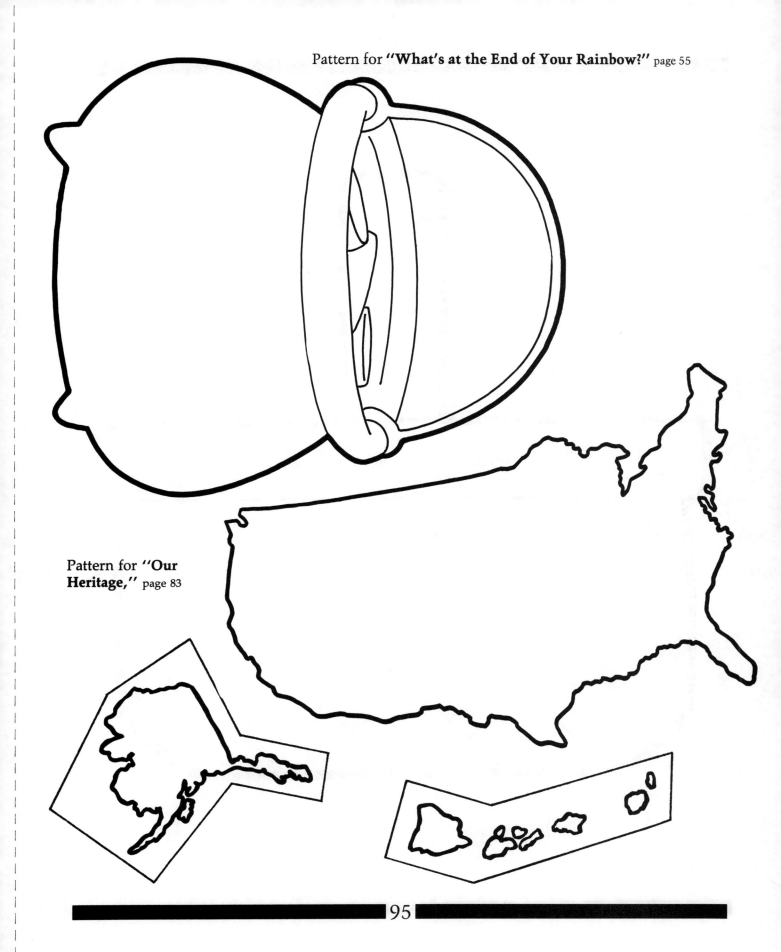

Pattern for **"Our Heritage,"** page 83

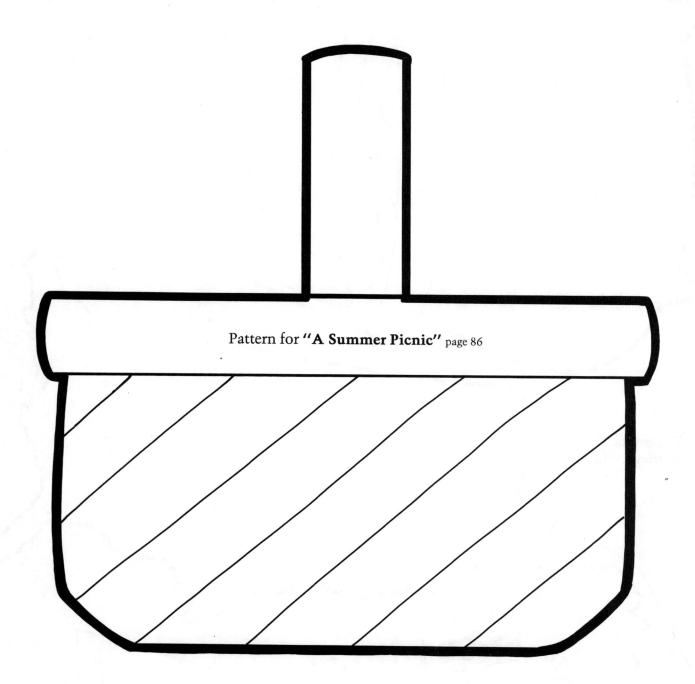

Pattern for **"A Summer Picnic"** <small>page 86</small>

Border Crossing

pieced by Donna Perrotta, appliqued by Janice Irick
quilted by Julie Lawson
Multiple borders create a wonderful frame for this center block. By mixing pieced and solid borders you can change a simple quilt into a real show stopper.

This stunning quilt offers a wonderful opportunity to experiment with borders and border prints. Create your masterpiece with these simple techniques.

FABRIC USED: "American Primer" by Minick & Simpson

instructions on pages 28 - 30

Market Square

pieced by Donna Hansen
quilted by Sue Needle

This lovely quilt gets its energy and visual interest by setting the center on point. With our technique, you don't have to be a math whiz to add the corners.

FABRIC USED: "Portobello Market" by 3 Sisters

instructions on pages 36 - 40

Pretty Poppies

*pieced by Donna Hansen
appliqued by Donna Perrotta
quilted by Sue Needle*

*When you really love flowers,
make them large! This design rule
worked for Georgia O'Keefe and it
will work for you. Pretty poppies
float across a soft pastel background that is so quick to assemble.*

*Large appliqué shapes with
smooth edges make this a wonderful choice for the novice quilter.*

FABRIC USED:
"Urban Couture" by Basic Grey

instructions on pages 48 - 51

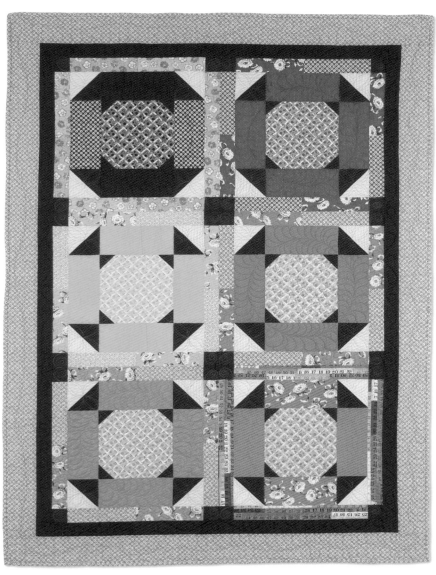

pieced by
Betty Nowlin
quilted by
Sue Needle

FABRIC USED:
"Recess" by
American Jane

instructions on
pages 44 - 45

Twist & Turn

   Twist and Turn mixes retro fabrics with traditional design for a neat new look. This back-to-basics style presents bold graphic lines that complement modern home decor while primary colors preserve a playful spirit.

   Perfect for the family room, game room, or kid's bedroom, this quilt is sure to find its way all over the house.

Leaves of Fall

pieced by Kayleen Allen
quilted by Julie Lawson
When summer's breezes give way to autumn's gusts, we are blessed with the magic of falling leaves. Celebrate the season with an abundance of rich color in this sensational quilt.

FABRIC USED: "Fabulous Fall" by Deb Strain

instructions on pages 46 - 47

Stars Across the Prairie

pieced by Donna Perrotta
quilted by Julie Lawson
Serene and naturally beautiful, neutral colors complement every décor all year long and are particularly favored by the men in your family, so this quilt is a must-do for the den, family room or guest room.

FABRIC USED: "Heritage - Cause for the Cure" by Howard Marcus

instructions on pages 41 - 43

*pieced by
Donna Perrotta
appliqued by
Janice Irick
quilted by
Julie Lawson*

FABRIC USED:
"Cotton Blossoms"
by Bonnie of Cotton
Way and Camille of
Thimble Blossoms

Big Barn

In this rushed age of deadlines, cell phones and congested commutes to work, little seems more appealing than getting back to the quiet calm of life on the farm.

Now you can capture the romance of an American icon with a quilt that brings to mind a peaceful Pennsylvania farm.

instructions on pages 52 - 57

*pieced by
Janice Irick*

*quilted by
Julie Lawson*

FABRIC USED:
"Louisa" by Terry
Clothier Thompson

Birds in the Garden

*Fill your garden with captivating birdsongs,
pretty flowers and a cute bunny. The 19th century
reproduction prints complement today's modern
decor beautifully.*

instructions on pages 58 - 61

Blooms in the Garden

pieced by Donna Perrotta
quilted by Julie Lawson

*All things bright and bloom-
ing… in every petal color! This gorgeous bed-size quilt invites you to
snuggle under a field of flowers.*

FABRIC USED:
"Woodland Bloom" by Lila Tueller
instructions on pages 62 - 64

Pretty in Pink

pieced by Betty Nowlin
appliqued by Janice Irick
quilted by Sue Needle

From streaks in the sunset to the rosy cheeks of our loved ones, we are surrounded daily by pretty shades of our favorite color.

Experienced quilters will find that altering the color palette gives this design a completely different attitude and a fabulous new look.

This beginner's favorite is a delightful indulgence in shades of Pink. This quilt goes together quickly and the applique flowers need no patterns - just cut your favorite shapes from leftover border scraps.

FABRIC USED: "Charisma" by Chez Moi
instructions on pages 66 - 67

Square by Square

pieced by Betty Nowlin
quilted by Sue Needle

Many of us began quilting by sewing squares together. This small quilt provides the beginner with an opportunity to make a stunning quilt. Fabric placement gives a rich pattern and interesting movement while the center shows off your favorite large scale print.

FABRIC: "Heritage - Cause for the Cure"

instructions on page 65

Star Crossed Pillow

Use leftover fabrics to make this fabulous complement for your Star-Crossed quilt.

Remember this one next time you need a quick Father's Day gift.

instructions
on page 71

Star Crossed

pieced by Lanelle Herron
quilted by Julie Lawson

Capture the serenity and peace of a quiet walk in the woods with a quilt whose construction won't leave you star crossed. This fabulous design will attract all the men in the family as well as campers, fishermen, hunters and everyone who loves the great outdoors.

Whether this quilt ends up in the den, family room or motor home, it's destined to be a favorite.

FABRIC: "Pine Creek Crossing" by Holly Taylor

instructions on pages 68 - 70

Big Bouquet

pieced by Kayleen Allen
appliqued by Janice Irick
quilted by susan Corbett

Every bed in the house deserves a fabulous quilt. Your guests will feel extra special when they find a gorgeous quilt on the bed. Quilts evoke a wide range of warm and fuzzy feelings including precious memories and they soften decor, inviting us to rest.

Big Bouquet is a beautiful quilt to include in your collection of family treasures.

FABRIC USED:
"Wildflower Serenade"
by Kansas Troubles

instructions on pages 19 - 23

Windowbox Flowers

pieced by Donna Arends Hansen
appliqued by Janice Irick
quilted by Julie Lawson

Anyone who has enjoyed an evening stroll through the garden knows that many flowers are fragrant after sunset.

Imagine moonbeams highlighting the soil in which these flowers are planted as you drift into slumber each night.

instructions on pages 24 - 27

Big Bouquet

photo is on page 18

SIZE: 70" x 79"
TIP: Add more borders to make a larger quilt.

YARDAGE:

Yardage is given for using either fabric yardage or
    'Layer Cake' squares.
We used a *Moda* "Wildflower Serenade" by Kansas Troubles
    'Layer Cake' collection of 10" x 10" fabric squares
    - we purchased 1 'Layer Cake'

9 squares	OR	⅞ yard Tan
6 squares	OR	⅝ yard Black
5 squares	OR	⅝ yard Red
5 squares	OR	⅝ yard Medium Blue
5 squares	OR	⅝ yard Navy
5 squares	OR	⅝ yard Green
4 squares	OR	⅓ yard Brown

Center A	Purchase ⅞ yard Tan
Border #3	Purchase ½ yard Green
Border #4 & Binding	Purchase 2 yards Tan
Backing	Purchase 5½ yards
Batting	Purchase 79" x 88"

Sewing machine, needle, thread
DMC Dark Green pearl cotton or 6-ply floss
#22 or #24 chenille needle
Black ½" button for bird's eye

PREPARATION FOR SQUARES:
    Cut all squares 10" x 10".
    Label the stacks or pieces as you cut.

SORTING:
    Sort the following 10" x 10" squares into stacks:

POSITION	QUANTITY & COLOR
B	1 Tan
C	4 Red
D	4 Medium Blue
E	2 Tan
F	2 Navy
G	4 Green
H	6 Black
I	4 Tan
K	1 Tan
L	3 Brown
M	1 Tan
N	2 Navy
O	1 Brown
Applique	1 Medium Blue
Applique	1 Navy
Applique	1 Green
Applique	1 Red

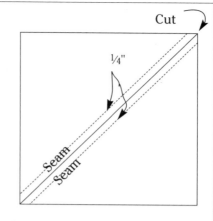

Half-Square Triangle Diagram
1. Place 2 squares right sides together.
2. Draw a diagonal line from corner to corner.
3. Stitch ¼" on each side of the line.
4. Cut squares apart on the diagonal line.
5. Open the 2 new squares with 2 colors.
6. Press. Trim off dog-ears.
7. Center and trim to size.

HALF-SQUARE TRIANGLES C-D:
Match the following squares for the half-square triangles:
    4 pairs of Red - Medium Blue
Follow the instructions in the Half-Square Triangle Diagram
    to make 8 half-square triangles.
Trim to 9½" x 9½".

CUTTING:
Cut and label the following pieces:

Center A:	Cut 1 square from yardage 27½" x 27½"
Snowball Corners B:	Cut 4 Tan squares 5" x 5"
Rectangles E:	Cut 4 Tan rectangles 5" x 9½"
Rectangles F:	Cut 4 Navy rectangles 5" x 9½"
Squares G:	Cut 4 Green squares 9½" x 9½"
Rectangle H:	Cut 6 Black rectangles 9½" x 10"
Rectangle I:	Cut 4 Tan rectangles 9½" x 10"
Square K:	Cut 2 Tan rectangles 5" x 10"
Rectangle L:	Cut 6 Brown rectangles 5" x 10"
Rectangle M:	Cut 4 Tan rectangles 2½" x 10"
Rectangle N:	Cut 3 Navy rectangles 5" x 10"
Rectangle O:	Cut 2 Brown rectangles 3¼"x 10"

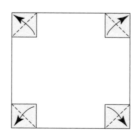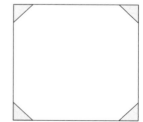

Snowball Corners Diagram

SEW BLOCKS:
Center: Refer to the Snowball Corners Diagram.
    Align a square B with each corner.
    Draw a diagonal line as shown and sew on the line.
    Fold the corner back and press. Repeat for all corners.

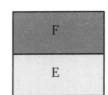

CENTER SIDE BLOCKS:
Block E-F:
    Sew E to F. Press.
    Trim to 9½" x 9½". Make 4.

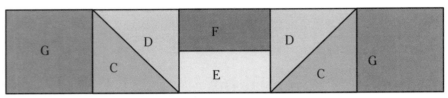

Top Section

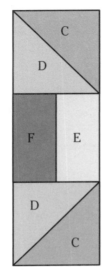

Left Center Section

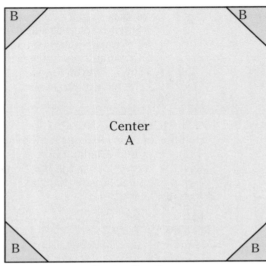

Center Section

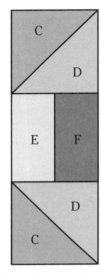

Right Center Section

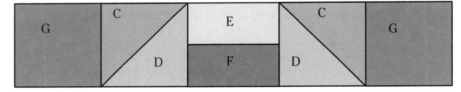

Bottom Section

Section Assembly Diagrams

SECTION ASSEMBLY:
    Arrange all blocks on a work surface or table.
    Refer to Section Assembly diagrams for block placement and direction.

SIDE SECTION ASSEMBLY:
Side Sections:
Note the position of the half-square triangles and block E-F.
    Sew C/D- E/F- D/C to make a piece 9½" x 27½". Press.
    Make 2.
    Sew a Side section to each side of Center A. Press.
Top & Bottom Sections:
Repeat for Bottom Section, noting the position of the half-square triangles and block E-F.
    Sew G- C/D -E/F- D/C- G. Press.
    Sew rows together. Press.
    Sew a section to the top and to the bottom of Center A. Press.

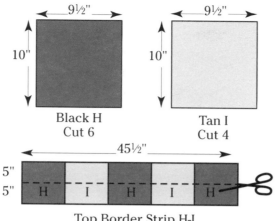

Black H
Cut 6

Tan I
Cut 4

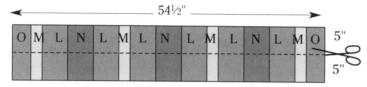

Top Border Strip H-I

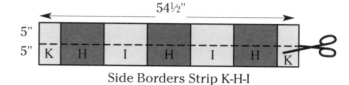

Side Borders Strip K-H-I

Pieced Top & Bottom Border #1:
Sew H-I-H-I-H. Press. The piece will measure 10" x 45½".
Cut the piece into 2 strips 5" x 45½".
Sew a strip to the top and bottom of the quilt. Press.

Pieced Side Border #1:
Sew K-H-I-H-I-H-K. Press. The piece will measure 10" x 54½".
Cut the piece into 2 strips 5" x 54½".
Sew a Side border to each side of the quilt. Press.

Top and Bottom Border Strips

Pieced Border #2 for Top and Bottom:
Sew O- M- L- N- L- M- L- N- L-M- L- N- L- M- O. Press. The piece will measure 10" x 54½".
Cut the piece into 2 strips 5" x 54½".
Sew a strip to the top and bottom of the quilt. Press.

Border #3:
Cut strips 2½" by the width of fabric.
Sew strips together end to end.
   Cut 2 strips 2½" x 63½" for sides.
   Cut 2 strips 2½" x 58½" for top and
   bottom.
   Sew side borders to the quilt. Press.
   Sew top and bottom borders to the
   quilt. Press.

Outer Border #4:
Cut strips 6½" wide parallel to the selvage
to eliminate piecing.
   Cut 2 strips 6½" x 67½" for sides.
   Cut 2 strips 6½" x 70½" for top and
   bottom.
   Sew side borders to the quilt. Press.
   Sew top and bottom borders to the
   quilt. Press.

APPLIQUE DESIGNS:
Applique: Refer to the Basic Instructions.
   Cut out the shapes using patterns
   and applique as desired.
   Embroider the stems using a long and
   short Running stitch.

FINISHING:
Quilting: See Basic Instructions.
Binding: Cut strips 2½" wide.
   Sew together end to end to
   equal 310".
   See Binding Instructions.

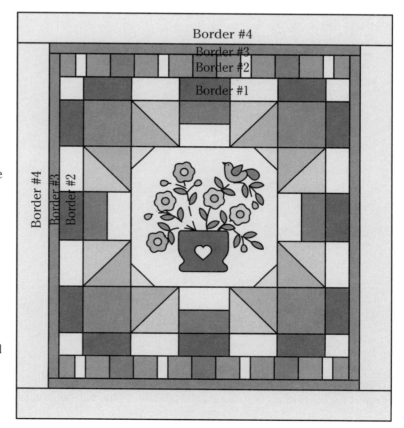

Big Bouquet - Quilt Assembly Diagram

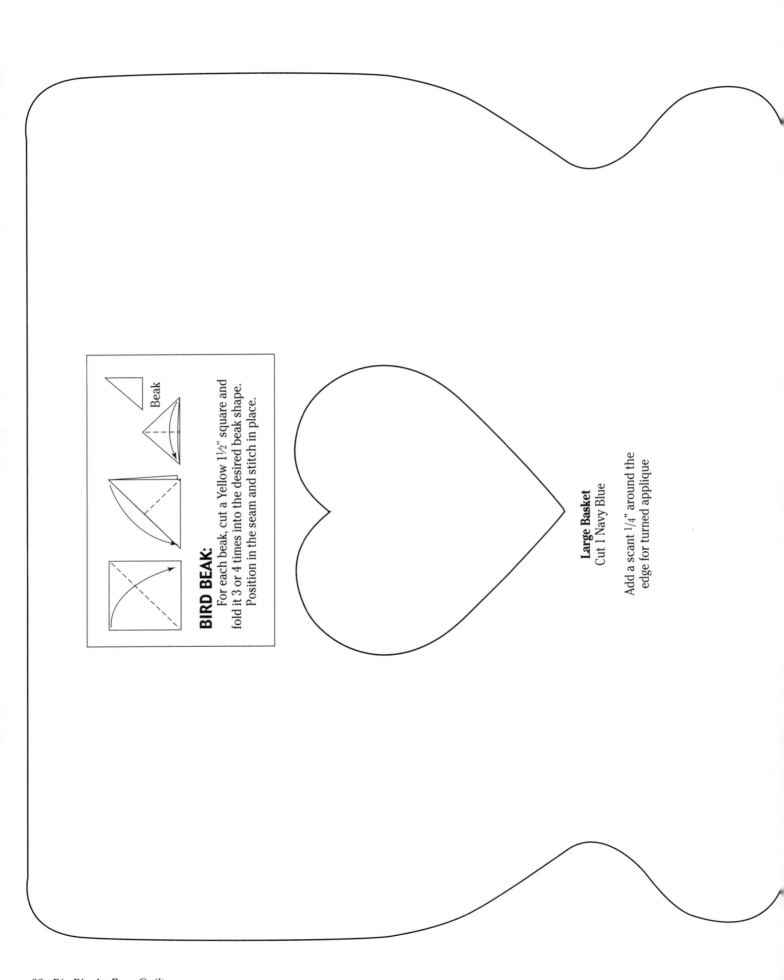

BIRD BEAK:

For each beak, cut a Yellow 1½" square and fold it 3 or 4 times into the desired beak shape. Position in the seam and stitch in place.

Beak

Large Basket
Cut 1 Navy Blue

Add a scant ¼" around the edge for turned applique

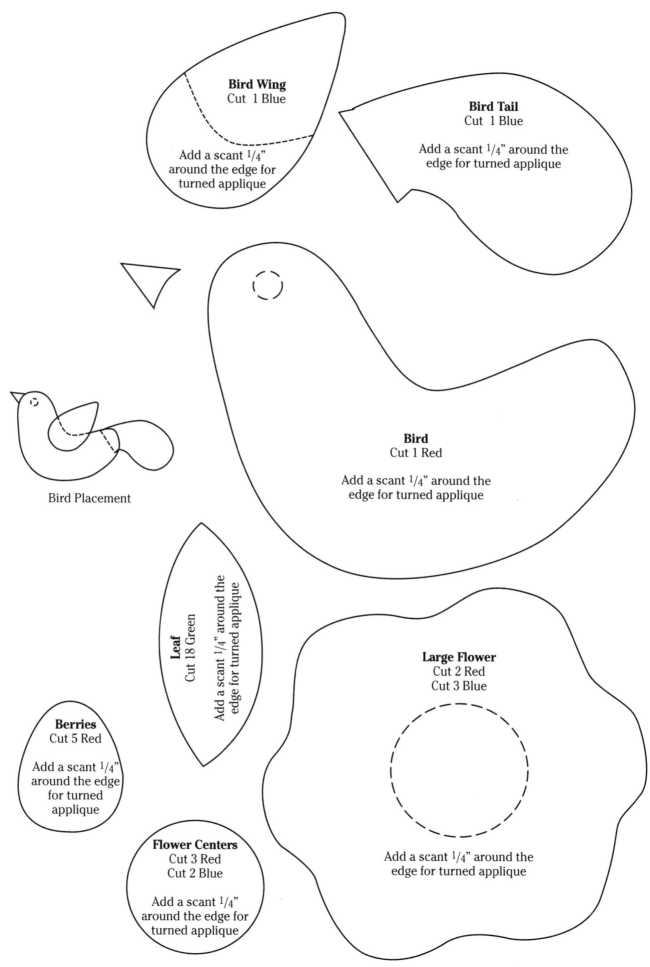

Bird Wing
Cut 1 Blue

Add a scant 1/4"
around the edge for
turned applique

Bird Tail
Cut 1 Blue

Add a scant 1/4" around the
edge for turned applique

Bird
Cut 1 Red

Add a scant 1/4" around the
edge for turned applique

Bird Placement

Leaf
Cut 18 Green

Add a scant 1/4" around the
edge for turned applique

Large Flower
Cut 2 Red
Cut 3 Blue

Add a scant 1/4" around the
edge for turned applique

Berries
Cut 5 Red

Add a scant 1/4"
around the edge
for turned
applique

Flower Centers
Cut 3 Red
Cut 2 Blue

Add a scant 1/4"
around the edge for
turned applique

Big Blocks Easy Quilts 23

Windowbox Flowers

photo is on page 18

SIZE: 68½" x 76½"
TIP: Add more borders to make a larger quilt.

YARDAGE:
Yardage is given for using either fabric yardage or
  'Layer Cake' squares.
We used a *Moda* "Wildflower Serenade" by Kansas Troubles
  'Layer Cake' collection of 10" x 10" fabric squares
  - we purchased 1 'Layer Cake'

6 squares	OR	⅝ yard Black
5 squares	OR	⅝ yard Navy
5 squares	OR	⅝ yard Forest Green
5 squares	OR	⅝ yard Burgundy
4 squares	OR	⅓ yard Brown
5 squares	OR	⅝ yard Medium Blue
9 squares	OR	⅞ yard Tan

Border #1	Purchase ½ yard Tan
Border #2 & Binding	Purchase 2 yards Black print
Backing	Purchase 5⅓ yards
Batting	Purchase 77" x 85"

Sewing machine, needle, thread
DMC pearl cotton or 6-ply floss
#22 or #24 chenille needle

PREPARATION FOR SQUARES:
  Cut all squares 10" x 10".
  Label the stacks or pieces as you cut.

SORTING: Sort the following 10" x 10" squares into stacks:

POSITION	QUANTITY & COLOR	
1, 7, 43, 49	1	Forest Green
3, 29, 35, 45	2	Forest Green
19,	1	Forest Green
2, 14, 36, 48	2	Navy
26, 38	2	Navy
4, 42	1	Black
12, 16, 20, 24, 32	5	Black
5, 15, 21, 47	2	Med. Blue
17, 31, 33	3	Med. Blue
6, 22, 28, 44	2	Burgundy
10, 40	2	Burgundy
8, 46	1	Brown
18, 30, 34	3	Brown
9, 11, 13, 23, 25, 27, 37, 39, 41	9	Tan
Set aside for appliques:	1	Navy
	1	Forest Green
	1	Burgundy

CUTTING:
Cut	1	Forest Green square into 4 squares 5" x 5" for #1, 7, 43, & 49.
Cut	2	Forest Green squares into strips 5" x 10" for #3, 29, 35, & 45.
Cut	2	Navy squares into strips 5" x 10" for #2, 14, 36, & 48.
Cut	1	Black square into strips 5" x 10" for #4, & 42.
Cut	2	Medium Blue squares into strips 5" x 10" for #5, 15, 21, & 47.
Cut	2	Burgundy squares into strips 5" x 10" for #6, 22, 28, & 44.
Cut	1	Brown square into strips 5" x 10" for #8, & 46.
Cut	2	Black strips 4½" x 57" for the top and bottom sashings.

			Outer Border #2			
			Inner Border #1			
			Top Sashing			
Block #1 Green	Block #2 Navy	Block #3 Forest Green	Block #4 Black	Block #5 Med. Blue	Block #6 Burgundy	Block #7 Green
Block #8 Brown	Block #9 Tan	Block #10 Burgundy	Block #11 Tan	Block #12 Black	Block #13 Tan	Block #14 Navy
Block #15 Med. Blue	Block #16 Black	Block #17 Med. Blue	Block #18 Brown	Block #19 Forest Green	Block #20 Black	Block #21 Med. Blue
Block #22 Bur-gundy	Block #23 Tan	Block #24 Black	Block #25 Tan	Block #26 Navy	Block #27 Tan	Block #28 Bur-gundy
Block #29 Forest Green	Block #30 Brown	Block #31 Med. Blue	Block #32 Black	Block #33 Med. Blue	Block #34 Brown	Block #35 Forest Green
Block #36 Navy	Block #37 Tan	Block #38 Navy	Block #39 Tan	Block #40 Burgundy	Block #41 Tan	Block #42 Black
Block #43 Green	Block #44 Burgundy	Block #45 Forest Green	Block #46 Brown	Block #47 Med. Blue	Block #48 Navy	Block #49 Green
			Bottom Sashing			

Windowbox Flowers - Quilt Assembly Diagram

ASSEMBLY:
Arrange all blocks on a work surface or table.
Refer to Quilt Assembly diagram for block placement and
  direction.
Sew blocks together in 7 rows, 7 blocks per row. Press.
Sew rows together. Press.
Sew sashing strips to the top and bottom of the quilt. Press.

APPLIQUE:
Cut out applique pieces from patterns.
See Applique Instructions.
Embroider stems with a long and short Running stitch.

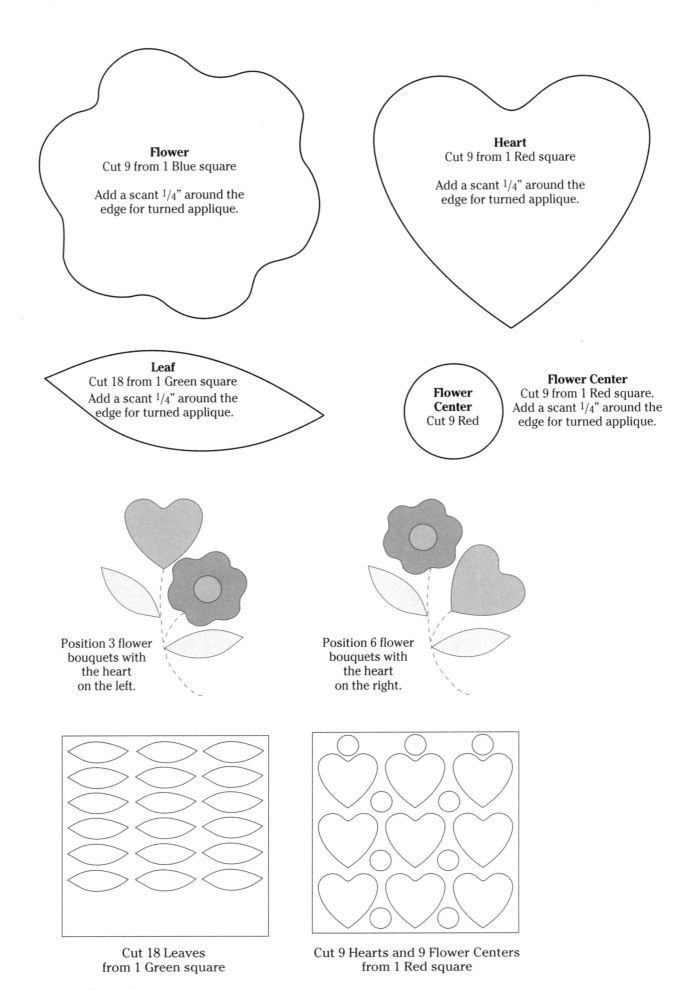

Flower
Cut 9 from 1 Blue square

Add a scant 1/4" around the
edge for turned applique.

Heart
Cut 9 from 1 Red square

Add a scant 1/4" around the
edge for turned applique.

Leaf
Cut 18 from 1 Green square
Add a scant 1/4" around the
edge for turned applique.

**Flower
Center**
Cut 9 Red

Flower Center
Cut 9 from 1 Red square.
Add a scant 1/4" around the
edge for turned applique.

Position 3 flower
bouquets with
the heart
on the left.

Position 6 flower
bouquets with
the heart
on the right.

Cut 18 Leaves
from 1 Green square

Cut 9 Hearts and 9 Flower Centers
from 1 Red square

Wildflower Serenade with Appliques

BORDERS:
Inner Border #1:
Cut strips 2½" by the width of fabric.
Sew strips together end to end.
    Cut 2 strips 2½" x 65" for sides.
    Cut 2 strips 2½" x 61" for top and bottom.
    Sew side borders to the quilt. Press.
    Sew top and bottom borders to the quilt. Press.

Outer Border #2:
Cut strips 4½" wide parallel to the selvage to eliminate piecing.
    Cut 2 strips 4½" x 69" for sides.
    Cut 2 strips 4½" x 69" for top and bottom.
    Sew side borders to the quilt. Press.
    Sew top and bottom borders to the quilt. Press.

FINISHING:
Quilting: See Basic Instructions.
Binding: Cut strips 2½" wide.
    Sew together end to end to equal 300".
    See Binding Instructions.

Border Crossing

photo is on pages 4 - 5

SIZE: 73" x 91"
TIP: Add more borders to make a larger quilt.

YARDAGE:
Yardage is given for using either fabric yardage or
    'Layer Cake' squares.
We used a *Moda* "American Primer" by Minick & Simpson
'Layer Cake' collection of 10" x 10" fabric squares
- we purchased 1 'Layer Cake'

11 squares	OR	⅞ yard White
7 squares	OR	⅝ yard Navy
6 squares	OR	⅝ yard Light Blue
4 squares	OR	⅓ yard Green
4 squares	OR	⅓ yard Red
2 squares	OR	⅓ yard Golden Brown
2 squares	OR	⅓ yard Border print

Center Block A	Purchase 1¼ yards White print
Border #2, #5 & Binding	Purchase 1½ yards Red
Border #4	Purchase 2⅛ yards Tan Border print
Border #6	Purchase 2⅜ yards White Border print
Backing	Purchase 6 yards
Batting	Purchase 81" x 99"

Sewing machine, needle, thread
DMC pearl cotton or 6-ply floss
#22 or #24 chenille needle

PREPARATION FOR SQUARES:
    Cut all squares 10" x 10".
    Label the stacks or pieces as you cut.

SORTING:
    Sort the following 10" x 10" squares into stacks:

POSITION	QUANTITY & COLOR
Block B	6 Navy, 6 White
Block C	4 Light Blue, 4 White
Block D	2 Red, 2 Light Blue
Block E	1 Navy plaid
Appliques	2 Golden Brown, 1 Navy Border print, 3 Green, 2 Red
Border #1	1 White, 1 Border print, 1 Green

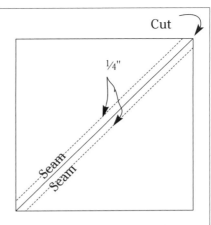

Half-Square Triangle Diagram
1. Place 2 squares right sides together.
2. Draw a diagonal line from corner to corner.
3. Stitch ¼" on each side of the line.
4. Cut squares apart on the diagonal line.
5. Open the 2 new squares with 2 colors.
6. Press. Trim off dog-ears.
7. Center and trim to size.

HALF-SQUARE TRIANGLES:
Pair up the following squares for half-square triangles:
    6 pairs of Navy - White for Block B's
    4 pairs of Light Blue - White for Block C's
    2 pairs of Light Blue - Red for Block D's
Follow the instructions in the Half-Square Triangle
    Diagram to make 24 half-square triangles.
Center and trim to 9½" x 9½".

CUTTING:
Block A:	Cut 1 White print 32½" x 41½" for the center
Block E:	Cut 4 Navy plaid squares 4¼" x 4¼"
Border #1:	Cut 1 Tan border print 10" x 10"

APPLIQUE:

Cut out all pieces from patterns.
Refer to the Basic Instructions. Applique as desired.
Embroider the stems with a long and short
    Running stitch.

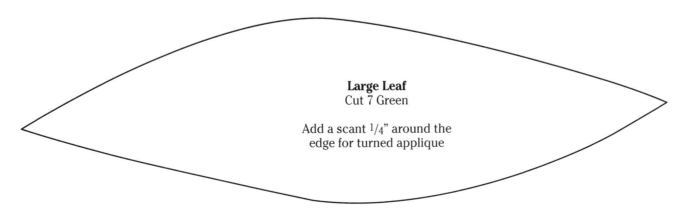

Large Leaf
Cut 7 Green

Add a scant ¼" around the
edge for turned applique

ASSEMBLY AND BORDERS:

Border #1:
You need the following 10" squares:
- 1 Green
- 1 White
- 1 Border print A
- 1 Tan Border print

Cut each square into 2 pieces, each 5" x 8½".
Sew the rectangles together end to end to make a piece 5" x 32½". Make 2. Press.

Top Row:
Sew one unit to the top of the center Block A. Press.

Bottom Row:
Sew one unit to the bottom of the center Block A. Press.

Small Center of Large Flower and Small Flower
Cut 3 Red
Cut 3 Blue

Add a scant ¹/₄" around the edge for turned applique.

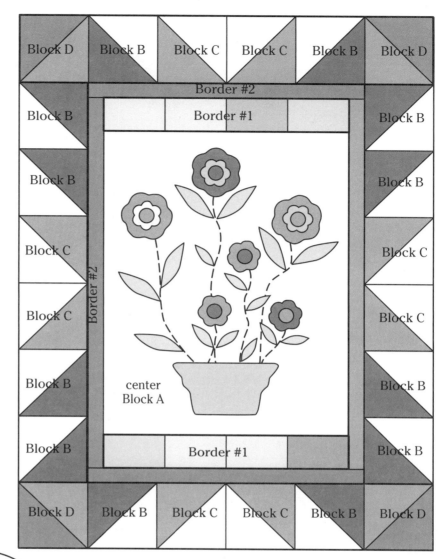

Border Crossing - Assembly Assembly

Small Flower
Cut 2 Red
Cut 1 Blue

Add a scant ¹/₄" around the edge for turned applique.

Border #2:
Cut strips 2½" by the width of fabric.
Sew strips together end to end.
- Cut 2 strips 2½" x 50½" for sides.
- Cut 2 strips 2½" x 36½" for top and bottom.
Sew side borders to the quilt. Press.
Sew top and bottom borders to the quilt. Press.

Half-Square Triangle Border #3:
Arrange all blocks on a work surface or table.
Refer to diagram for block placement.

Side borders:
Sew blocks B-B-C-C-B-B. Press. Make 2.
Top/Bottom borders:
Sew blocks D-B-C-C-B-D. Press. Make 2.

Sew side borders to the quilt. Press.
Sew top and bottom borders to the quilt. Press.

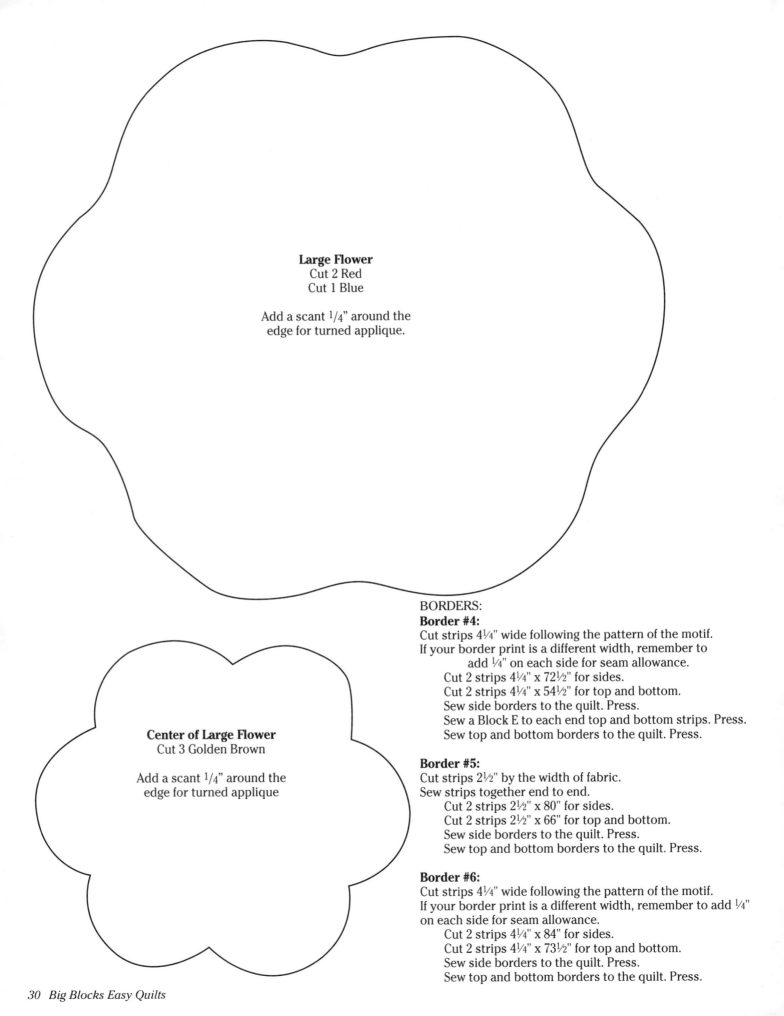

Large Flower
Cut 2 Red
Cut 1 Blue

Add a scant ¹/₄" around the
edge for turned applique.

Center of Large Flower
Cut 3 Golden Brown

Add a scant ¹/₄" around the
edge for turned applique

BORDERS:
Border #4:
Cut strips 4¼" wide following the pattern of the motif.
If your border print is a different width, remember to
add ¼" on each side for seam allowance.
Cut 2 strips 4¼" x 72½" for sides.
Cut 2 strips 4¼" x 54½" for top and bottom.
Sew side borders to the quilt. Press.
Sew a Block E to each end top and bottom strips. Press.
Sew top and bottom borders to the quilt. Press.

Border #5:
Cut strips 2½" by the width of fabric.
Sew strips together end to end.
Cut 2 strips 2½" x 80" for sides.
Cut 2 strips 2½" x 66" for top and bottom.
Sew side borders to the quilt. Press.
Sew top and bottom borders to the quilt. Press.

Border #6:
Cut strips 4¼" wide following the pattern of the motif.
If your border print is a different width, remember to add ¼"
on each side for seam allowance.
Cut 2 strips 4¼" x 84" for sides.
Cut 2 strips 4¼" x 73½" for top and bottom.
Sew side borders to the quilt. Press.
Sew top and bottom borders to the quilt. Press.

Border #6

Border #5

Border #4

E

E

Border #6

Border #5

Border #4

FINISHING:
Quilting:
See Basic Instructions.

Binding:
Cut strips 2½" wide.

Sew together end to end to equal 338".

See Binding Instructions.

E

E

Border Crossing - Borders Assembly

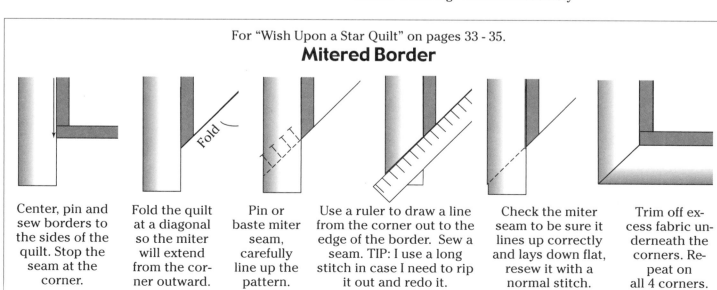

For "Wish Upon a Star Quilt" on pages 33 - 35.
Mitered Border

Center, pin and sew borders to the sides of the quilt. Stop the seam at the corner.	Fold the quilt at a diagonal so the miter will extend from the corner outward.	Pin or baste miter seam, carefully line up the pattern.	Use a ruler to draw a line from the corner out to the edge of the border. Sew a seam. TIP: I use a long stitch in case I need to rip it out and redo it.	Check the miter seam to be sure it lines up correctly and lays down flat, resew it with a normal stitch.	Trim off excess fabric underneath the corners. Repeat on all 4 corners.

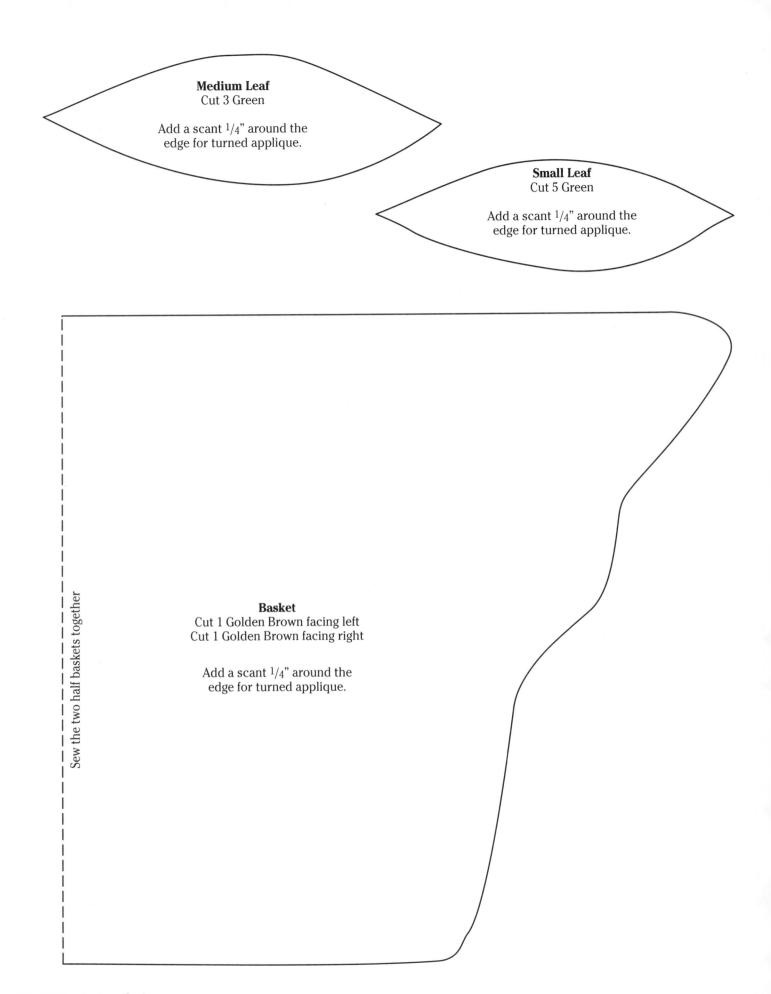

Medium Leaf
Cut 3 Green

Add a scant 1/4" around the
edge for turned applique.

Small Leaf
Cut 5 Green

Add a scant 1/4" around the
edge for turned applique.

Basket
Cut 1 Golden Brown facing left
Cut 1 Golden Brown facing right

Add a scant 1/4" around the
edge for turned applique.

Sew the two half baskets together

Wish Upon A Star

photo is on page 4

SIZE: 67½" x 67½"

TIP: Add more borders to make a larger quilt.

YARDAGE:

Yardage is given for using either fabric yardage or
    'Layer Cake' squares.
We used a *Moda* "American Primer" by Minick & Simpson
    'Layer Cake' collection of 10" x 10" fabric squares
    - we purchased 1 'Layer Cake'

12 squares	OR	⅞ yard White
6 squares	OR	⅝ yard Light Blue
5 squares	OR	⅝ yard Navy
3 squares	OR	⅓ yard Red
2 squares	OR	⅓ yard Border Prints
2 squares	OR	⅓ yard Golden Brown
1 square	OR	⅓ yard Green

Border #4	Purchase ⅜ yard Red
Border #5 & Binding	Purchase 2 yards Border print
Backing	Purchase 4⅛ yards
Batting	Purchase 75" x 75"

Sewing machine, needle, thread

PREPARATION FOR SQUARES:
    Cut all squares 10" x 10".
    Label the stacks or pieces as you cut.

SORTING:
    Sort the following 10" x 10" squares into stacks:

POSITION	QUANTITY & COLOR
Center Blocks A:	2 Border prints, 2 Golden Brown

Border #1:	Block B:	2 Light Blue, 2 Red
	Block C:	1 White
	Block D:	1 White, 1 Red

Border #2:		3 Navy

Border #3:	Block E:	4 White, 4 Light Blue
	Block F:	2 White, 2 Navy
	Block G:	4 White
	Block H:	1 Green

CUTTING:
    Cut 4 White squares 4½" x 4½" for C.
    Cut 4 White squares 9½" x 9½" for G.
    Cut 4 White and 4 Navy rectangles 5" x 8½" for F.
    Cut 8 Green strips 1½" x 9½" for H.
    Cut 11 Navy strips 2½" x 10" for Border #2.

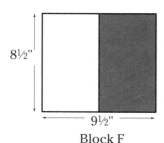

8½" 9½"

Block F

BLOCK F:
Refer to the Block F
diagram.
Sew a Navy and White
rectangle together to
make a piece
8½" x 9½".
Press.
Make 4.

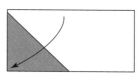

Align a square with the end of the strip. Draw a diagonal
line and sew on the line. Fold back the triangle.

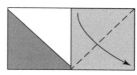

Repeat on the other end of the strip. Press.

Flying Geese Diagram

FLYING GEESE FOR BORDER #1:
    Cut 4 Light Blue rectangles 4½" x 8½".
    Cut 8 Red squares 4½" x 4½".

    Refer to the Flying Geese instructions above.
    Draw a diagonal line as shown. Sew on the line and fold back
        the triangle. Press.
    Repeat for all corners. Make 4 blocks.

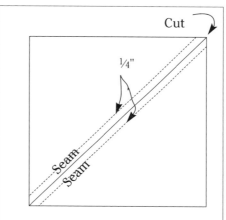

Cut

¼"

Seam
Seam

Half-Square Triangle Diagram
1. Place 2 squares right sides together.
2. Draw a diagonal line from corner to corner.
3. Stitch ¼" on each side of the line.
4. Cut squares apart on the diagonal line.
5. Open the 2 new squares with 2 colors.
6. Press. Trim off dog-ears.
7. Center and trim to size.

HALF-SQUARE
TRIANGLES FOR
THE CENTER A:
    Cut 2 Border Print
and 2 Golden Brown
squares 9" x 9".
    Match 2 pairs of
Print-Golden Brown.
    Follow the instruc-
tions in the Half-
Square Triangle
Diagram to make 4
half-square triangles.
    Trim to 8½" x 8½".

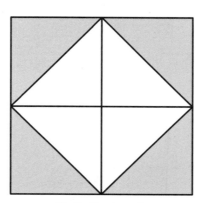

Quilt Center A

ASSEMBLE CENTER A:
    Arrange half-square tri-
angles in 2 rows of 2 with
the Border Print triangles in
the center.
    Sew the blocks together.
Press.
    Sew the rows together.
Press.
    The center will measure
16½" x 16½".

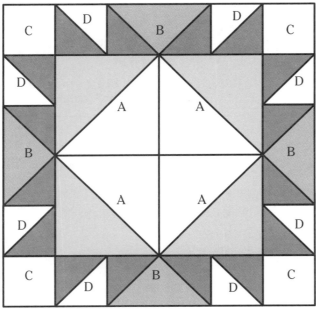

Border #1

HALF-SQUARE TRIANGLES FOR BORDER #1:
 Cut 4 White and 4 Red squares 5" x 5".
 Match 4 pairs of White-Red.
 Follow the instructions in the Half-Square
  Triangle Diagram to make 8 half-square
  triangles. Trim to 4½" x 4½".

HALF-SQUARE TRIANGLES FOR BORDER #3:
 Match 4 pairs of White-Light Blue 10" squares.
 Follow the instructions in the Half-Square
  Triangle Diagram to make 8 half-square
  triangles. Trim to 9½" x 9½".

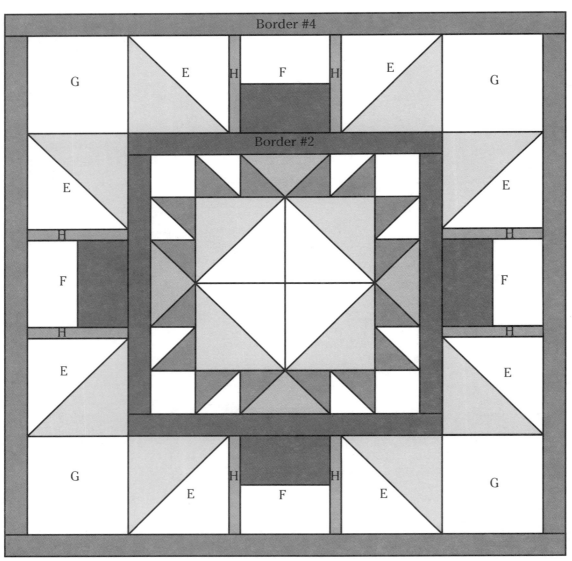

Border #3

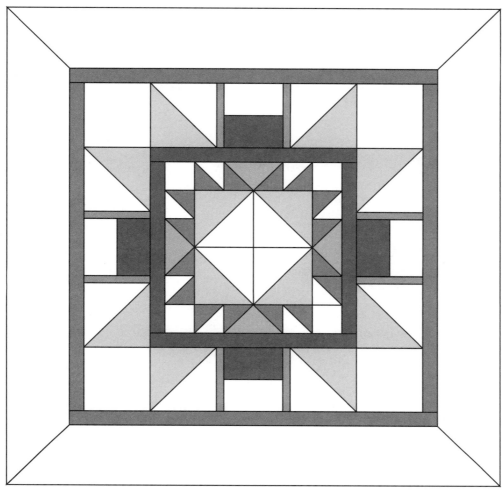

Wish Upon A Star - Quilt Assembly Diagram

ASSEMBLY:
Arrange all blocks on a work surface or table.
Refer to diagram for block placement
and direction.
Sew all blocks and strips together.

BORDERS:
Border #1:
Refer to the Border #1 Diagram for placement and direction.
Sides:
Sew D-B-D. Press. Make 2.
Sew sides to the center piece. Press.

Top/Bottom:
Sew C-D-B-D-C. Press. Make 2.
Sew the top and bottom borders to the center piece. Press.
The block will measure 24½" x 24½" at this point.

Border #2:
Sew Navy border strips end to end. Press.
Cut 2 strips 2½" x 24½" for the sides.
Cut 2 strips 2½" x 28½" for the top and bottom.
Sew side borders to the quilt. Press.
Sew top and bottom borders to the quilt. Press.

Border #3:
Refer to the Border #3 diagram for direction and placement.
Sides: Sew E-H-F-H-E. Press. Make 2.
Sew side borders to the quilt. Press.
Top/Bottom: Sew G-E-H-F-H-E-G. Press.
Sew top and bottom borders to the quilt. Press.

Border #4:
Cut strips 2½" by the width of fabric.
Sew strips end to end. Press.
Cut 2 strips 2½" x 46½" for sides.
Cut 2 strips 2½" x 50½" for top and bottom.
Sew side borders to the quilt. Press.
Sew top and bottom borders to the quilt. Press.

Border #5:
Refer to the Mitered Border instructions on page 31.
Our border print was 8¾" wide so we cut our strips 9¼" wide.
Cut 2 strips 9¼" x 72" for sides.
Cut 2 strips 9¼" x 72" for top and bottom.
Sew side borders to the quilt. Press.
Sew top and bottom borders to the quilt. Press.
Miter the corners.

FINISHING:
Quilting: See Basic Instructions.
Binding: Cut strips 2½" wide.
Sew together end to end to equal 280".
See Binding Instructions.

Market Square

photo is on page 6

SIZE: 68" x 77"
TIP: Add more borders to make a larger quilt.

YARDAGE:
Yardage is given for using either fabric yardage or
    'Layer Cake' squares.
We used a *Moda* "Portobello Market" by 3 Sisters
    'Layer Cake' collection of 10" x 10" fabric squares
    - we purchased 1 'Layer Cake'

7 squares	OR	⅝ yard Ivory
7 squares	OR	⅝ yard Tan
7 squares	OR	⅝ yard Rose
6 squares	OR	⅝ yard Medium Blue
5 squares	OR	⅝ yard Brown
4 squares	OR	⅓ yard Light Blue
2 squares	OR	⅓ yard Green

Border #1	Purchase ½ yard Green
Border #2	Purchase ½ yard Dark Brown
Border #3 & Binding	Purchase 2¼ yards Brown print
Backing	Purchase 5¼ yards
Batting	Purchase 76" x 85"
Sewing machine, needle, thread	

PREPARATION FOR SQUARES:
    Cut all squares 10" x 10".
    Label the stacks or pieces as you cut.

SORTING:
    Sort the following 10" x 10" squares into stacks:

POSITION	QUANTITY & COLOR
Inner Square	
A	4 Ivory
B	4 Tan
C	4 Dark Rose
D	3 Dark Rose
E	1 Tan
F	4 Light Blue
Unit G	1 Ivory, 1 Brown
H	2 Ivory
Corners	
I-J	2 Medium Blue, 4 Brown, 2 Green, 1 Tan with Rose
K-L	4 Medium Blue, 4 Brown, 1 Tan

CUTTING CHART

	Quantity	Length	Position
Center Section			
Ivory	4	9½" x 9½"	A
	2	5" x 10"	G
	4	5" x 9½"	H
Tan	8	5" x 9½"	B
Tan with Rose print	2	5" x 9½"	E
Rose	16	5" x 5"	C
	6	5" x 9½"	D
Light Blue	16	5" x 5"	F
Brown	2	5" x 10"	G

Corner Section
Cut all pieces 9½" x 9½":

6 Medium Blue for	#1, 9, 10, 12, 16, 18
2 Green for	#3, 7
2 Tan for	#5, 14
4 Brown for	#4, 6, 13, 15
From Brown Border #3 fabric, cut 4 for	#2, 8, 11, 17

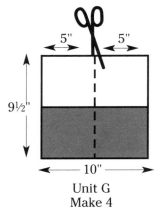

Unit G
Make 4

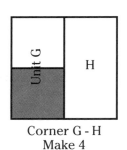

Corner G - H
Make 4

BLOCKS FOR CENTER SECTION:
Corner G-H:
    Refer to the Unit G diagram.
    Sew an Ivory strip G to a Brown strip G to make a
        piece 9½" x 10". Press.
    Cut the piece into 2 units 5" x 9½".
    Repeat for the remaining G strips. Make 4 G units.
    Refer to the Corner G-H diagram.
    Sew Unit G to H. Press. Make 4.
    Each block will measure 9½" x 9½" at this point.

FLYING GEESE:

Refer to the Flying Geese Diagram to make units:

8 B-C
6 D-F
2 E-F

For B-C:

Align a Rose square C on one end of Tan strip B. Draw the diagonal and sew on the line. Fold back the flap and press. Repeat for the other end.

For D-F:

Repeat B-C instructions using Light Blue squares and Rose strips.

For E-F:

Repeat B-C instructions using Light Blue squares and Tan with Rose print strips.

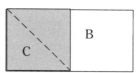
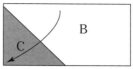

Align a square with the end of the block. Sew a diagonal line as shown. Fold back the triangle. Press.

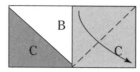
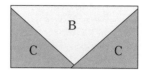

Align a square with the other end of the block. Sew a diagonal line as shown. Fold back the triangle. Press.

Flying Geese Diagrams

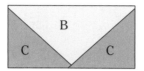

Make 8 of B-C

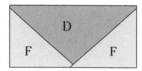

Make 6 of D-F

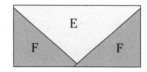

Make 2 of E-F

ZIG ZAG STRIPS ASSEMBLY:

Border Assembly:

Refer to the Center Section diagram for block placement and direction.

Refer to the Center Section diagram for block placement and direction.

Side Strips:

Sew 2 B-C geese end to end to make a strip 5" x 18½".

Sew 2 D-F geese end to end to make a strip 5" x 18½".

Sew the strips together to make a piece 9½" x 18½". Make 2.

Top & Bottom Strips:

Sew 2 B-C geese end to end to make a strip 5" x 18½".

Sew a D-F to an E-F end to end to make a strip 5" x 18½".

Sew the strips together to make a piece 9½" x 18½". Make 2.

CENTER SECTION ASSEMBLY:

Arrange all blocks on a work surface or table. Refer to diagram for block placement.

Center:

Sew blocks A together in 2 rows, 2 blocks per row. Press.

Sew rows together. Press.

Side Borders:

Sew the Left and Right Flying Geese sections to the left and right sides of the Center. Press.

Top & Bottom Borders:

Sew a Corner G-H on each end of the remaining Flying Geese sections, paying attention to the direction of the diagonals and position of G-H. Press.

Sew a border strip to the top and bottom of the Center. Press.

The Center section will measure 36½" x 36½" at this point.

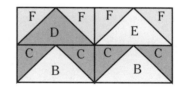
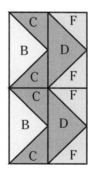

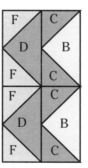

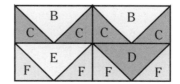
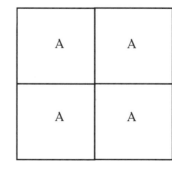

Center Section Diagram

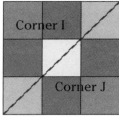

Corners I & J
Block Assembly

Corners I & J
Cutting Diagram

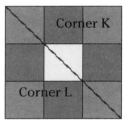

Corners K & L
Block Assembly

Corners K & L
Cutting Diagram

BLOCKS FOR CORNER SECTION:

Arrange the blocks on a work surface or table.

Refer to Corner Section diagram for block placement.

For each Corner Section, sew 3 rows, 3 blocks per row.

Press.

Sew rows together. Press.

Draw a diagonal line on I-J and K-L as shown.

Sew a ⅛" Stay stitch on each side of the line.

This will preserve the shape of the bias edge and prevent stretching.

Cut on the diagonal line. Label the pieces.

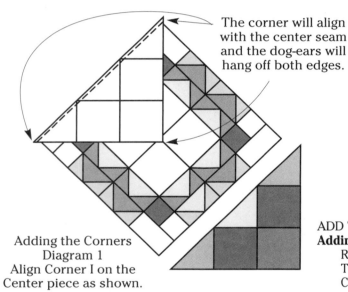

The corner will align with the center seam and the dog-ears will hang off both edges.

Adding the Corners
Diagram 1
Align Corner I on the
Center piece as shown.

ADD THE CORNERS:

Adding the Corners:

Refer to the Adding Corners diagram.

Turn the Center section on point as shown.

Center and pin Corners I & J to the upper left and lower right of the Center section.

The point of the corner will align with the center seam.

Sew and press leaving the dog-ears in place.

Center and pin Corners K & L to the upper right and lower left corners. Sew and press.

Trim the dog-ears.

Adding the Corners
Diagram 2
Align Corner J on the
Center piece as shown.

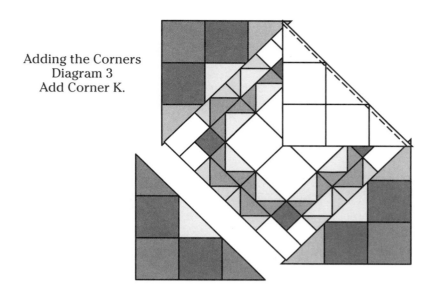

Adding the Corners
Diagram 3
Add Corner K.

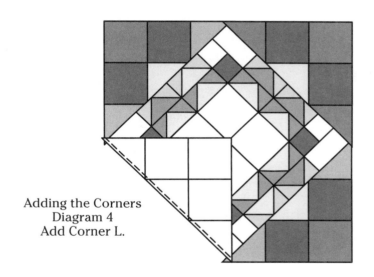

Adding the Corners
Diagram 4
Add Corner L.

Finished Center with Corners

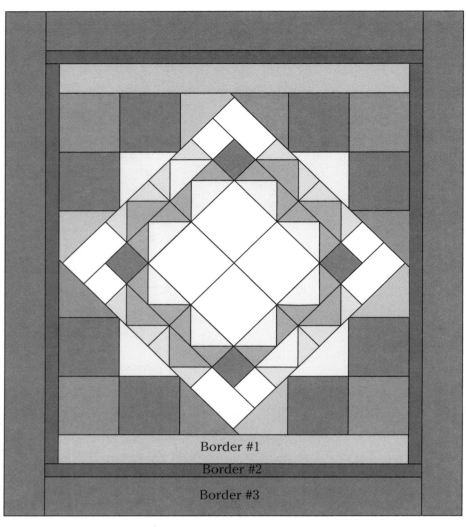

Market Square - Quilt Assembly

BORDERS:
Border #1:
Cut strips 5" by the width of fabric.
Sew strips together end to end.
    Cut 2 strips 5" x 52½" for top and bottom.
    Sew top and bottom borders to the quilt. Press.

Border #2:
Cut strips 2½" by the width of fabric.
Sew strips together end to end.
    Cut 2 strips 2½" x 61½" for sides.
    Cut 2 strips 2½" x 56½" for top and bottom.
    Sew side borders to the quilt. Press.
    Sew top and bottom borders to the quilt. Press.

Border #3:
Cut strips 6½" wide parallel to the selvage to eliminate piecing.
    Cut 2 strips 6½" x 77½" for sides.
    Cut 2 strips 6½" x 56½" for top and bottom.
    Sew top and bottom borders to the quilt. Press.
    Sew side borders to the quilt. Press.

FINISHING:
Quilting: See Basic Instructions.
Binding: Cut strips 2½" wide.
    Sew together end to end to equal 301".
    See Binding Instructions.

Stars Across the Prairie

photo is on pages 10 - 11

SIZE: 57" x 66"
TIP: Add more borders to make a larger quilt.

YARDAGE:
Yardage is given for using either fabric yardage or
    'Layer Cake' squares.
We used a *Moda* "Heritage, Cause for the Cure" by Howard Marcus
    'Layer Cake' collection of 10" x 10" fabric squares
    - we purchased 1 'Layer Cake'

8 squares	OR	⅝ yard Dark Brown
8 squares	OR	⅝ yard Brown
8 squares	OR	⅝ yard Tan
4 squares	OR	⅓ yard Light Blue-Gray
3 squares	OR	⅓ yard Paisley or print
2 squares	OR	⅓ yard Medium Blue-Gray
2 squares	OR	⅓ yard Dark Blue-Gray
2 squares	OR	⅓ yard Rose

Borders #1 & 3 & Binding Purchase 2 yards Tan
Borders #1 & 2   Purchase ½ yard Dark Brown
Backing   Purchase 3⅓ yards
Batting   Purchase 65" x 74"
Sewing machine, needle, thread

PREPARATION FOR SQUARES:
    Cut all squares 10" x 10".
    Label the stacks or pieces as you cut.

SORTING:
    Sort the following 10" x 10" squares into stacks:

POSITION	QUANTITY & COLOR
A	1 Rose
B	1 Rose
C	2 Dark Blue-Gray
D	8 Dark Brown
E	8 Brown
F	8 Tan
G	3 Paisley
H	4 Light Blue-Gray
I	2 Medium Blue-Gray

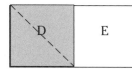

Align a square with the end of the block. Sew a diagonal line as shown. Fold back the triangle. Press.

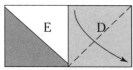
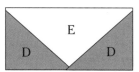

Align a square with the other end of the block. Sew a diagonal line as shown. Fold back the triangle. Press.

Flying Geese Diagrams

FLYING GEESE:
    Label the pieces as you cut.
Cutting for Flying Geese Block D/E:
    D   cut 32 Dark Brown squares   5" x 5"
    E   cut 16 Brown strips   5" x 9½"
Refer to the Flying Geese Diagram to make
    16 Flying Geese sections.

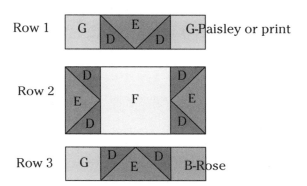

Star Block
Make 4

STAR BLOCKS:
    Make 4.
Cutting for Center and Corners:
    For Center   F   cut 4 Tan squares   9½" x 9½"
    For Corners   G   cut 12 Paisley or print 5" x 5"
    For Corners   B   cut 4 Rose squares   5" x 5"
Assembly:
    Refer to the Star Block diagram for placement.

Row 1:
    Sew G - D/E - G. Press.
    Make 1 for each block,
        for a total of 4.
Row 2:
    Sew D/E - F - D/E. Press.
    Make 1 for each block,
        for a total of 4.
Row 3:
    Sew G - D/E - B. Press.
    Make 1 for each block,
        for a total of 4.
Assembly:
    Sew the rows together. Press.
    Each block will measure 18½" x 18½" at this point.

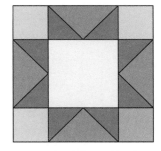

Finished Star Block

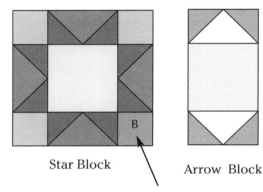

Row 1 I | I-Med. Blue-Gray
Row 2 F
Row 3 C | C-Dark Blue-Gray

Arrow Block
Make 4

ARROW BLOCKS:
Make 4.

Cutting for Arrow Center squares:

| For centers | F | cut 4 Tan squares | 9½" x 9½" |

Cutting for Flying Geese Blocks H/C and H/I:

For Arrow blocks	C	cut 8 Dark Blue-Gray squares	5" x 5"
For Arrow blocks	I	cut 8 Med. Blue-Gray squares	5" x 5"
For Arrow blocks	H	cut 8 Light Blue-Gray strips	5" x 9½"

Refer to the Flying Geese Diagram to make
4 Flying Geese sections with H/C and
4 Flying Geese sections with H/I and

Assembly:
Refer to Arrow Block diagram for placement.
For each block, sew an H/I to the top of F. Press.
Sew an H/C to the bottom of F. Press.
Each block will measure 9½" x 18½" at this point.

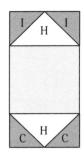

I | H | I
H
C | H | C

Finished
Arrow Block

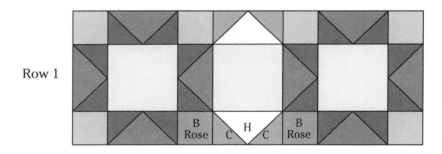

Star Block   Arrow Block

Note: The B square is darker. Position all B squares in the center of the quilt.

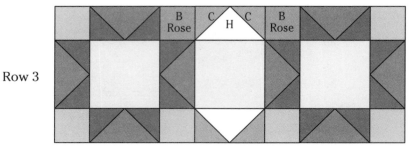

Row 1

Row 2

Row 3

Row Assembly Diagram

ASSEMBLY:
Cutting for Center square:
For quilt center A, cut 1 Rose square
9½" x 9½".
Assemble the Quilt:
Arrange all blocks on a work surface or
table.
Refer to diagram for block placement and
direction.
Note the position of the Rose square B in
each Star block.
Note the position of each H/C in each
Arrow block.

Sew blocks together in 3 rows, 3 blocks
per row. Press.
Sew rows together. Press.

Stars Across the Prairie
Quilt Assembly Diagram

BORDERS:

Pieced Border #1:
Cut 6 strips 5" x 12½" from Tan yardage.
Cut 4 Dark Brown squares 5" x 5".
Sew pieces together end to end: Tan-Brown-Tan-Brown-Tan.
    Press. Make 2 strips 5" x 45½".
    Sew a strip to the top and bottom of the quilt. Press.

Inner Border #2:
Cut strips 2½" by the width of fabric.
Sew strips together end to end.
    Cut 2 strips 2½" x 54½" for sides.
    Cut 2 strips 2½" x 49½" for top and bottom.
    Sew side borders to the quilt. Press.
    Sew top and bottom borders to the quilt. Press.

Outer Border #3:
Cut strips 4½" wide parallel to the selvage to
    eliminate piecing.
    Cut 2 strips 4½" x 58½" for sides.
    Cut 2 strips 4½" x 57½" for top and bottom.
    Sew side borders to the quilt. Press.
    Sew top and bottom borders to the quilt. Press.

FINISHING:
Quilting: See Basic Instructions.
Binding: Cut strips 2½" wide.
    Sew together end to end to equal 256".
    See Binding Instructions.

Note: This quilt is also available as a pattern pack
    #0958 "Stars Across the Prairie"
    by Design Originals.

Twist & Turn

photo is on page 8

SIZE: 55" x 76½"

TIP: Add more borders to make a larger quilt.

YARDAGE:

Yardage is given for using either fabric yardage or
    'Layer Cake' squares.

We used a *Moda* "Recess" by American Jane
    'Layer Cake' collection of 10" x 10" fabric squares
    - we purchased 1 'Layer Cake'

2 squares	OR	⅓ yard Ruler print
3 squares	OR	⅓ yard Ivory
5 squares	OR	⅝ yard Light Blue
5 squares	OR	⅝ yard Yellow
4 squares	OR	⅓ yard Navy
5 squares	OR	⅝ yard Green
4 squares	OR	⅓ yard Orange
6 squares	OR	⅝ yard Red

Border #1 & B, D, G   Purchase 1 yard Navy
Border #2 & Binding   Purchase 2 yards Green print
Backing   Purchase 4¼ yards
Batting   Purchase 63" x 85"
Sewing machine, needle, thread

PREPARATION FOR SQUARES:

Cut all squares 10" x 10".
Label the stacks or pieces as you cut.

SORTING:

Sort the following 10" x 10" squares into stacks:

POSITION	QUANTITY	& COLOR
Block 6: F	2	Ruler print
Half-square triangles E	3	Ivory
Block 4: A, C, F	5	Light Blue
Block 3: A, C, F	5	Yellow
Block 1: A, C	4	Navy
Block 5: A, C, F	5	Green
Block 1: F, Block 6: A, C	4	Orange
Block 1: F; Block 2: A, C, F	6	Red

CUTTING:

For piece C, cut the following 4½" x 10" strips:
    4 Navy for Block 1
    4 Red for Block 2
    4 Yellow for Block 3
    4 Light Blue for Block 4
    4 Green for Block 5
    4 Orange for Block 6

For piece F, cut the following 2½" x 9¼":
    4 Orange & 4 Red for Block 1
        (Note: Use lightest Red & Orange for Block 1.)
    8 Red for Block 2
    8 Yellow for Block 3
    8 Light Blue for Block 4
    8 Green for Block 5
    8 Ruler print for Block 6

For Half-square triangles E, cut 12 Ivory 5" x 5" squares.

From Navy Border #1 fabric, cut the following:
    24 squares 2½" x 2½" for snowball corners B
    12 squares 5" x 5" for Half-square triangles D
    24 squares 2½" x 2½" for cornerstones G.

HALF-SQUARE TRIANGLES D/E:

Match the following squares for the half-square triangles:
    12 pairs of Ivory - Navy
Follow the instructions in the Half-square Triangle Diagram on the page
to the right to make 24 half-square triangles. Trim to 4½" x 4½".

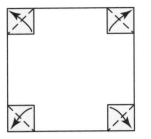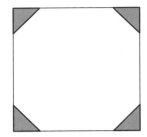

SEW BLOCKS:

Refer to the Snowball Corners diagram above.
For each block A, align a square B with each corner.
Draw a diagonal line as shown and sew on the line.
Fold the corner back and press. Repeat for all corners.

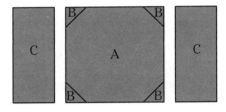

SEW C STRIPS TO BLOCKS:

Sew a strip C to the left and to the right sides of each block. Press.
Refer to the Block Assembly diagram.

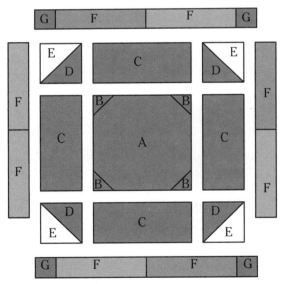

Block Assembly Diagram

SEW HALF-SQUARE TRIANGLES TO BLOCKS:

For each block, sew a half-square triangle D-E to each end of the
    remaining 2 strip C's. Press.
Sew a D/E - C - D/E strip to the top and bottom of each block.
    Press.
For each block, sew 4 sets of 2 F strips end to end.
Sew an F-F strip to the right and left sides of each block. Press.
Sew a cornerstone G to each end of the remaining F-F strips. Press.
Sew a G - F-F - G strip to the top and bottom of each block. Press.
Each block will measure 22" x 22" at this point.

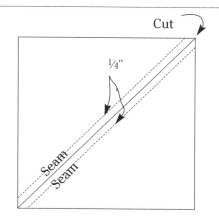

Cut

1/4"

Seam
Seam

Half-Square Triangle Diagram
1. Place 2 squares right sides together.
2. Draw a diagonal line from corner to corner.
3. Stitch 1/4" on each side of the line.
4. Cut squares apart on the diagonal line.
5. Open the 2 new squares with 2 colors.
6. Press. Trim off dog-ears.
7. Center and trim to size.

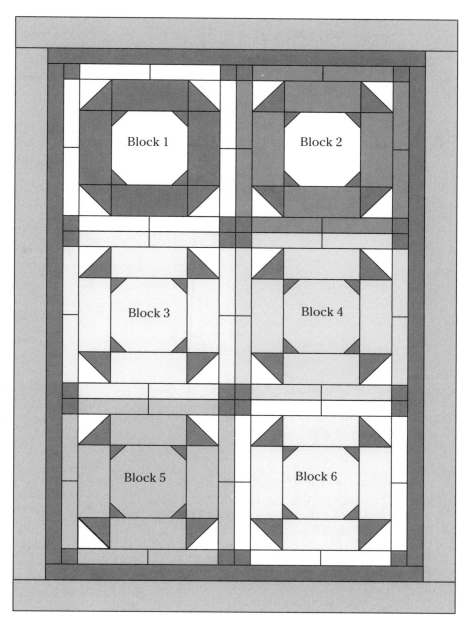

Block 1 Block 2

Block 3 Block 4

Block 5 Block 6

Twist & Turn - Quilt Assembly Diagram

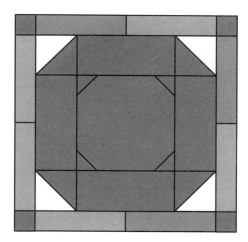

Finished Block

ASSEMBLY:
Arrange all blocks on a work surface or table.
Refer to diagram for block placement and direction.
Sew blocks together in 3 rows, 2 blocks per row. Press.
Sew rows together. Press.

Inner Border #1:
Cut strips 2½" by the width of fabric.
Sew strips together end to end.
Cut 2 strips 2½" x 65" for sides.
Cut 2 strips 2½" x 47½" for top and bottom.
Sew side borders to the quilt. Press.
Sew top and bottom borders to the quilt. Press.

Outer Border #2:
Cut strips 4½" wide parallel to the selvage to eliminate piecing.
Cut 2 strips 4½" x 69" for sides.
Cut 2 strips 4½" x 55½" for top and bottom.
Sew side borders to the quilt. Press.
Sew top and bottom borders to the quilt. Press.

FINISHING:
Quilting: See Basic Instructions.
Binding: Cut strips 2½" wide.
Sew together end to end to equal 274".
See Binding Instructions.

Leaves of Fall

photo is on page 9

SIZE: 60" x 68"
TIP: Add more borders to make a larger quilt.

YARDAGE:
Yardage is given for using either fabric yardage or
   'Layer Cake' squares.
We used a *Moda* "Fabulous Fall" by Deb Strain
   'Layer Cake' collection of 10" x 10" fabric squares
  - we purchased 1 'Layer Cake'

6 squares	OR	⅝ yard Tan
6 squares	OR	⅝ yard Teal
6 squares	OR	⅝ yard Red
4 squares	OR	⅓ yard Brown
4 squares	OR	⅓ yard Orange
3 squares	OR	⅓ yard Green
2 squares	OR	⅓ yard Gold

Border #2	Purchase ⅜ yard Green
Border #3	Purchase ⅜ yard Brown
Border #4 & Binding	Purchase 1¾ yards Tan
Backing	Purchase 3¾ yards
Batting	Purchase 68" x 76"

Sewing machine, needle, thread

PREPARATION FOR SQUARES:
   Cut all squares 10" x 10".
   Label the stacks or pieces as you cut.

SORTING:
   Sort the following 10" x 10" squares into stacks:

POSITION	QUANTITY & COLOR
A	1 Gold, 2 Green, 1 Brown
B	1 Tan, ½ Gold, 1 Green, ½ Orange 1 Brown
C	½ Tan, ¼ Orange, ¼ Brown
D	½ Tan, ¼ Orange, ¼ Brown
E	1 Tan, ½ Orange, ½ Brown
F	2 Tan, 1 Orange, 1 Brown
Border #1 Half-Square Triangles	6 Red, 6 Teal
Border #1 Cornerstones	1 Tan, 1 Orange

HALF-SQUARE TRIANGLES:
For Position B -
   Cut and label the following squares 5" x 5":
   Block 1: cut 2 Brown, 2 Green
   Block 2: cut 2 Tan, 2 Gold
   Block 3: cut 2 Brown, 2 Tan
   Block 4: cut 2 Orange, 2 Green

Match the following squares for the half-square triangles:
   2 pairs of Brown-Green for Block 1
   2 pairs of Tan-Gold for Block 2
   2 pairs of Brown-Tan for Block 3
   2 pairs of Orange-Green for Block 4

For Pieced Border #1 -
   Cut and label 24 Red and 24 Teal 5" x 5" squares.
Follow the instructions in the Half-Square Triangle
   Diagram at right to make 16 half-square triangles B
   and 48 Red-Teal for Pieced Border #1.
   Trim to 4½" x 4½".

CUTTING FOR BLOCKS:
Cut and label the following pieces:

Label	Size	Color, & Block #
A	8½" x 8½"	2 Green for blocks 1 & 4
		1 Gold for block 2
		1 Brown for block 3
C	4½" x 4½"	1 Brown for block 1
		2 Tan for blocks 2 & 3
		1 Orange for block 4
D	2½" x 4½"	2 Brown for block 1
		4 Tan for blocks 2 & 3
		2 Orange for block 4
E	2½" x 8½"	2 Brown for block 1
		4 Tan for blocks 2 & 3
		2 Orange for block 4
F	2½" x 8½"	4 Brown for block 1
		8 Tan for blocks 2 & 3
		4 Orange for block 4

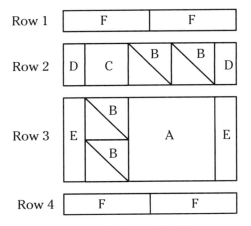

Block Assembly Diagram

BLOCK ASSEMBLY:
   Refer to the Block Assembly Diagram.
   Arrange all pieces on a work surface or table.
Rows 1 & 4: For each row, sew 2 F strips end to end.
   Make 2 pieces 2½" x 16½". Press.
Row 2: Sew D-C-B-B-D. Press.
Row 3: Sew 2 half-square triangles B together to make
    a piece 4½" x 8½". Press.
   Sew this strip to the left side of square A. Press.
   Sew a strip E to the right and left sides of the block.
   Press.
   Sew the rows together. Press.
   Make 4.
   Each block will measure 16½" x 16½" at this point.

Finished Block

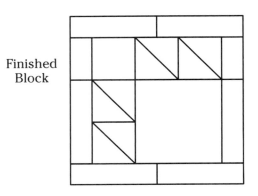

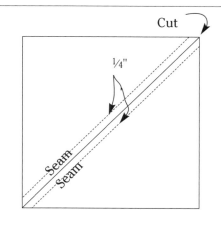

Half-Square Triangle Diagram
1. Place 2 squares right sides together.
2. Draw a diagonal line from corner to corner.
3. Stitch ¼" on each side of the line.
4. Cut squares apart on the diagonal line.
5. Open the 2 new squares with 2 colors.
6. Press. Trim off dog-ears.
7. Center and trim to size.

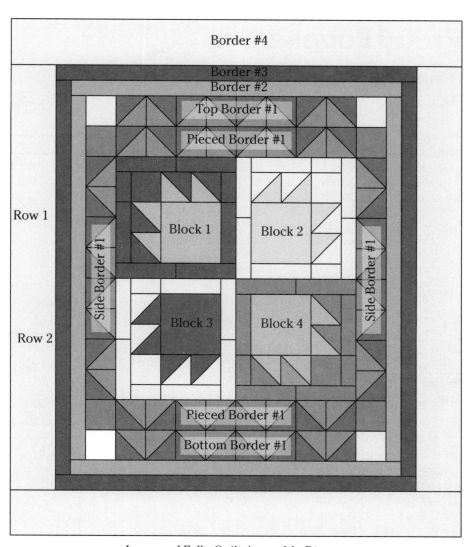

Leaves of Fall - Quilt Assembly Diagram

ASSEMBLY:

Arrange all blocks on a work surface or table.

Refer to diagram for block placement and direction.

Sew blocks together in 2 rows, 2 blocks per row. Press.

Sew rows together. Press.

BORDERS:

Pieced Borders #1:

Cut 4 Tan and 4 Orange cornerstone squares, each 4½" x 4½".
Refer to Quilt Assembly diagram for block placement and direction.
Sew 6 strips of 8 Red-Teal half-square triangles. Press.
The half-square triangle strip units will be 4½" x 32½".

Sew Side Borders #1:

Sew one half-square triangle strip unit to each side of the quilt (notice the direction of the triangles). Press.

Top & Bottom Borders #1:

Sew a Tan cornerstone square to each end of 2 half-square triangle strip units. Press.
Sew an Orange cornerstone square to each end of the 2 remaining half-square triangle strip units. Press.
Referring to the Quilt Assembly Diagram, sew 2 half-square triangle strip units together (one Tan with cornerstones, one with Orange cornerstones). Be sure to notice the direction of the triangles). Press.
Make 2 strip units 8½" x 40½".

Sew Top & Bottom Borders #1

Sew a border strip unit to the top of the quilt. Press.
Sew a border strip unit to the bottom of the quilt. Press.

Border #2:

Cut strips 2½" by the width of fabric.
Sew strips together end to end.
Cut 2 strips 2½" x 48½" for sides.
Cut 2 strips 2½" x 44½" for top and bottom.
Sew side borders to the quilt. Press.
Sew top and bottom borders to the quilt. Press.

Border #3:

Cut strips 2½" by the width of fabric.
Sew strips together end to end.
Cut 2 strips 2½" x 52½" for sides.
Cut 2 strips 2½" x 48½" for top and bottom.
Sew side borders to the quilt. Press.
Sew top and bottom borders to the quilt. Press.

Outer Border #4:

Cut strips 6½" wide parallel to the selvage to eliminate piecing.
Cut 2 strips 6½" x 56½" for sides.
Cut 2 strips 6½" x 60½" for top and bottom.
Sew side borders to the quilt. Press.
Sew top and bottom borders to the quilt. Press.

FINISHING:

Quilting: See Basic Instructions.
Binding: Cut strips 2½" wide.
Sew together end to end to equal 266".
See Binding Instructions.

Pretty Poppies

photo is on page 7

SIZE: 53" x 63"

TIP: Add more borders to make a larger quilt.

YARDAGE:

Yardage is given for using either fabric yardage or
    'Layer Cake' squares.

We used a *Moda* "Urban Couture" by Basic Grey
    'Layer Cake' collection of 10" x 10" fabric squares
    - we purchased 1 'Layer Cake'

9 squares	OR	⅞ yard Blue
8 squares	OR	⅝ yard Yellow
7 squares	OR	⅝ yard Green
7 squares	OR	⅝ yard Brown
5 squares	OR	⅝ yard Red

Border #3	Purchase ⅜ yard Dark Blue
Border #4 & Binding	Purchase 1⅝ yards Med. Blue
Backing	Purchase 3¼ yards
Batting	Purchase 64" x 72"

Sewing machine, needle, thread

PREPARATION FOR SQUARES:
    Cut all squares 10" x 10".
    Label the stacks or pieces as you cut.

SORTING:
    Sort the following 10" x 10" squares into stacks:

POSITION	QUANTITY & COLOR
A	7 Green, 5 Blue
B & C, D & E	5 Brown
Pieced Border 1	4 Blue
Pieced Border 2	5 Yellow
Appliques	5 Red, 3 Yellow, 2 Brown

CUTTING:

Cut and label the following pieces:

Blocks 1,3,4,6,8,10,12	Green squares 9½" x 9½"
Blocks 2,5,7,9,11	Blue squares 9½" x 9½"
Sashing B	12 Brown strips 1" x 9½"
Sashing C	12 Brown strips 1" x 10"
Sashing D	4 Brown strips 1" x 10"
Sashing E	4 Brown strips 1" x 10"
Pieced Border #1	15 Blue strips 2½" x 10"
Pieced Border #2	17 Yellow strips 2½" x 10"

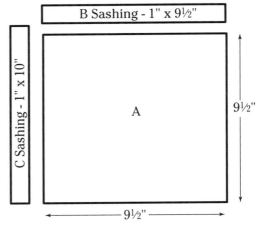

Block Diagram

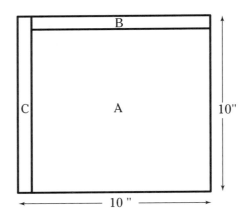

Finished Block

BLOCK ASSEMBLY:
    Sashing strip B
        Sew a 1" x 9½" to the top of each Block A.
        Press.
    Sashing strip C
        Sew a 1" x 10" to the left side of each Block A.
        Press.

ASSEMBLY:
    Arrange all blocks on a work surface or table.
    Refer to diagram for block placement and direction.
    Sew the blocks together in 4 rows (3 blocks per row).
    Press.
    Sew the rows together. Press.

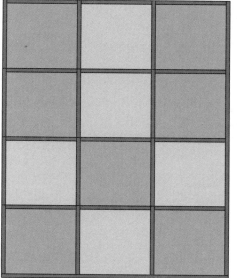

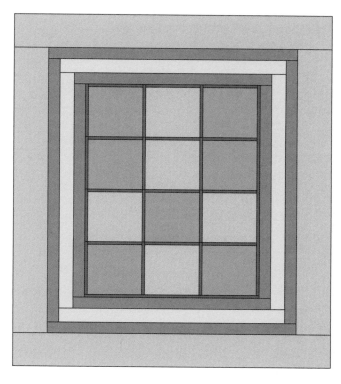

Sashing D - 1" x 38½"
Finished size of quilt at this point - 39"

Sashing E - 1" x 29½"
Finished size of quilt at this point - 29½"

Center of Quilt Diagram

ADD SIDE & BOTTOM SASHING:

Sashing D - Right Side:
Cut 4 strips, each 1" x 10".
Sew the 4 strips together end to end
to make a strip 1" x 38½".
Sew to the right side of the quilt. Press.

Sashing E - Bottom:
Cut 4 strips, each 1" x 8½".
Sew the 4 strips together end to end to make a
strip 1" x 32½"
Cut 3" off the end to make a strip 1" x 29½".
Sew to the bottom of the quilt. Press.

Pieced Border #1:
Sew Blue strips end to end. Press.
Cut 2 strips 2½" x 39" for sides.
Cut 2 strips 2½" x 33½" for top and bottom.
Sew side borders to the quilt. Press.
Sew top and bottom borders to the quilt. Press.

Pieced Border #2:
Sew Yellow strips end to end. Press.
Cut 2 strips 2½" x 43" for sides.
Cut 2 strips 2½" x 37½" for top and bottom.
Sew side borders to the quilt. Press.
Sew top and bottom borders to the quilt. Press.

Border #3:
Cut strips 2½" by the width of fabric.
Sew strips together end to end.
Cut 2 strips 2½" x 47" for sides.
Cut 2 strips 2½" x 41½" for top and bottom.
Sew side borders to the quilt. Press.
Sew top and bottom borders to the quilt. Press.

Border #4:
Cut strips 6½" wide parallel to the selvage to
eliminate piecing.
Cut 2 strips 6½" x 51" for sides.
Cut 2 strips 6½" x 53½" for top and bottom.
Sew side borders to the quilt. Press.
Sew top and bottom borders to the quilt. Press.

FINISHING:
Applique: See Basic Instructions.
Cut out shapes from patterns. Applique as desired.
Quilting: See Basic Instructions.
Binding: Cut strips 2½" wide.
Sew together end to end to equal 242".
See Binding Instructions.

Note: This quilt is also available as a pattern pack #0960
"Pretty Poppies" by Design Originals.

Pretty Poppies - Applique Assembly

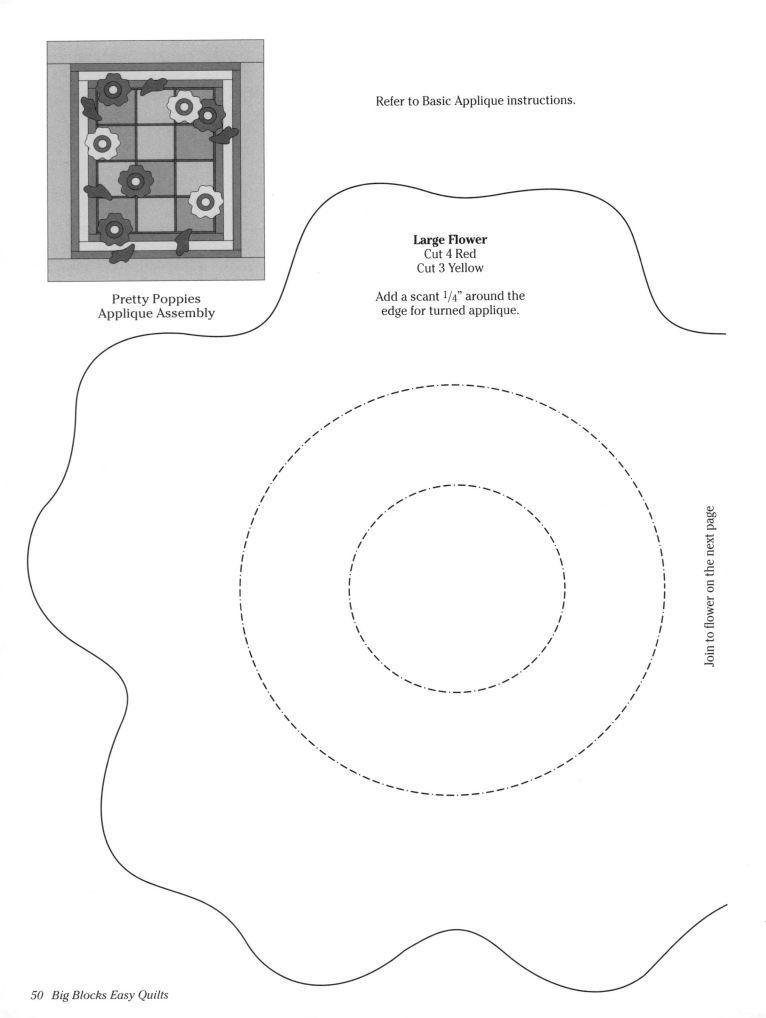

Refer to Basic Applique instructions.

Pretty Poppies
Applique Assembly

Large Flower
Cut 4 Red
Cut 3 Yellow

Add a scant 1/4" around the
edge for turned applique.

Join to flower on the next page

Small Flower Center
Cut 7 Yellow

Add a scant $1/4$" around the edge for turned applique.

Large Flower Center
Cut 3 Red
Cut 4 Brown

Add a scant $1/4$" around the edge for turned applique.

Join to flower on the previous page

Leaf
Cut 3 Brown - Left
Cut 3 Brown - Right

Add a scant $1/4$" around the edge for turned applique.

Big Barn

photo is on page 12

SIZE: 60" x 64"
TIP: Add more borders to make a larger quilt.

YARDAGE:
Yardage is given for using either fabric yardage or
    'Layer Cake' squares.
We used a *Moda* "Cotton Blossoms"
    by Bonnie of Cotton Way and Camille of Thimble Blossoms
    'Layer Cake' collection of 10" x 10" fabric squares
    - we purchased 1 'Layer Cake'

8 squares	OR	⅝ yard Red
8 squares	OR	⅝ yard Tan
8 squares	OR	⅝ yard Dark Brown
6 squares	OR	⅝ yard Green
4 squares	OR	⅓ yard Brown
2 squares	OR	⅓ yard Stripe
2 squares	OR	⅓ yard Red plaid
2 squares	OR	⅓ yard Green plaid

Border #2	Purchase ⅔ yard Green
Border #3 & Binding	Purchase 1¾ yards Dark Brown
Backing	Purchase 3½ yards
Batting	Purchase 68" x 72"

Sewing machine, needle, thread
DMC Brown pearl cotton or 6-ply floss
#22 or #24 chenille needle

PREPARATION FOR SQUARES:
    Cut all squares 10" x 10".
    Label the stacks or pieces as you cut.

SORTING:
    Sort the following 10" x 10" squares into stacks:

POSITION	QUANTITY & COLOR
Sections 3, 4, Sky	8 Tan
Sections 1, 2, 4, side borders	2 Red plaid, 2 Green Plaid
Section 4 Roof/Sky	2½ Dark Brown, 2 Stripe
Sections 1 & 2	5 Dark Brown, 4 Brown
Section 5	6 Green
Pieced Border #1	8 Red
Appliques	Dark Brown and Brown scraps from 10" squares and outer border

CUTTING FROM YARDAGE:
    4½" x 4½" Green squares:
        Cut 4 for Border #1 cornerstones.
        Cut 1 for applique.
    8½" x 9" Green rectangles:
        Cut 4 for Pieced Border #1.

CUTTING FROM 10" SQUARES:
Section 3: Cut 10 Tan squares 4½" x 4½".
Sections 1, 2, & 4: Plaid Side borders:
    Cut 4 Red and 4 Green strips 4½" x 8½"
Section 2: Sky
    Cut 8 Tan squares 4½" x 4½".
Solid squares for Roof/Sky section:
    Cut 6 Tan squares 4½" x 4½".
    Cut 6 Dark Brown squares 4½" x 4½".
    Cut 3 Stripe squares 4½" x 4½".
Sections 1 & 2:
    Cut 6 Dark Brown & 2 Brown 4½" x 4½" squares.
    Cut 3 Dark Brown & 2 Brown 8½" x 8½" squares.
    Cut 2 Brown 4½" x 8½" rectangles for barn doors.
Section 5: Cut 5 Green Layer Cakes into 10 strips 4½" x 9".
    Arrange the strips in 5 pairs.

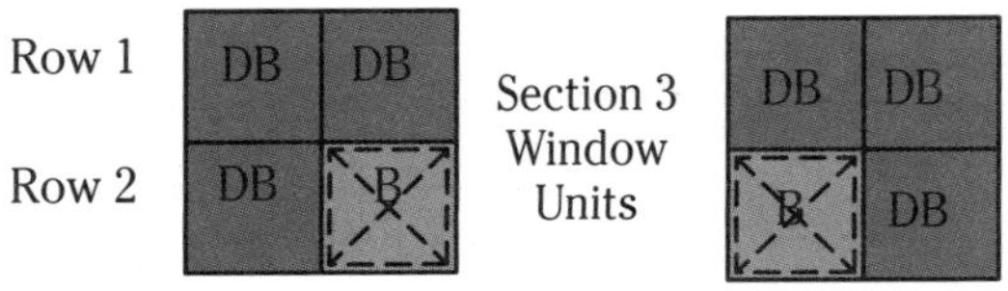

Section 1 – Window Units:
    Refer to the diagram for block placement.

Window Units:
    Row 1: Sew 2 Dark Brown (DB) squares together. Press.
    Row 2: Sew a Dark Brown (DB) and Brown (B) square
        together. Press.
    Sew the rows together to form a block 8½" x 8½".
    Press. Make 2.

Assembly for Window Section:
    Arrange the pieces on a work surface.
    Sew a Green plaid 4½" x 8½" strip- Window unit-Dark
Brown 8½" square-Window unit- Brown 8½" square- Red
plaid 4½" x 8½" strip.
    Press.

Section 2 – Door Section:
Assembly for Door Section:
    Sew a Green plaid 4½" x 8½" strip-Dark Brown 8½"
square - 2 Brown doors- Dark Brown 8½" square- Brown
8½" square- Red plaid 4½" x 8½" strip.
    Press.

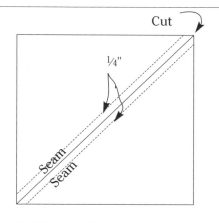

Half-Square Triangle Diagram
1. Place 2 squares right sides together.
2. Draw a diagonal line from corner to corner.
3. Stitch ¼" on each side of the line.
4. Cut squares apart on the diagonal line.
5. Open the 2 new squares with 2 colors.
6. Press. Trim off dog-ears.
7. Center and trim to size.

HALF-SQUARE TRIANGLES
FOR ROOF/SKY SECTION:
Cut 2 Brown and 2 Tan squares 5" x 5".
Match 2 pairs of Brown-Tan and follow the
    instructions for Half-Square Triangles to make 4
    Brown-Tan half-square triangles.
    You will use 3 of them. Trim to 4½" x 4½".

Striped Roof Section:
   NOTE: If you want all your stripes to run in the
same direction, you will not be able to construct the
half-square triangles using speed cutting techniques.

   Start by cutting a 5" square from template plastic.
Cut this square on one diagonal to make a triangle.
Use this as a pattern to cut 3 Brown and 3 Tan triangles.

   Handle these carefully to avoid stretching the bias.
   Position the triangles on a work surface and
plan the position of your stripes. Cut 6 stripe triangles
and match them with their Brown or Tan partners.
   Sew a scant ¼" seam along the longest side
(bias edge).
   Open the half-square triangle and press.
   Center and trim to 4½" x 4½".

Tan/Brown   Brown/Stripe   Stripe/Tan
Make 3   Make 3   Make 3

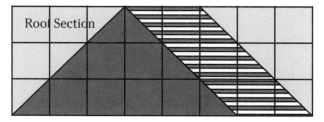

The roof section will use half square triangles.
(See below in Section 3 - Sky & Roof.)

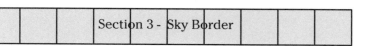

SKY SECTION ASSEMBLY:
Section 3 – Sky Border:
   Sew 10 Tan squares together to make a strip
4½" x 40½". Press.

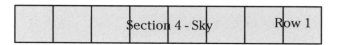

Section 4 – Sky:
   Sew 8 Tan squares together to make a strip
4½" x 32½". Press.

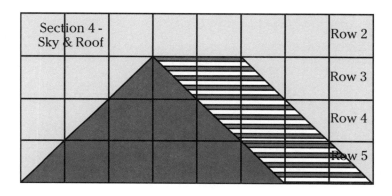

Section 4 – Sky & Roof:
   Refer to the diagram for block placement.
   Sew 3 rows of 8 squares. Press.

   Sew Rows 2 and 3 together. Press.
   Sew Rows 4 and 5 together. Press.

   Sew these 2 units together. Press.

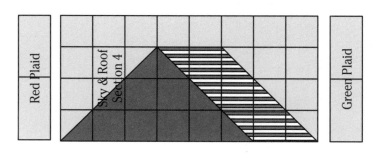

Sew 2 Red plaid 4½" x 8½" strips together end to end
    to make a strip 4½" x 16½".
Sew 2 Green plaid 4½" x 8½" strips together end to
    end to make a strip 4½" x 16½".
Sew the Red plaid 4½" x 16½" on the left side. Press.
Sew the Green plaid 4½" x 16½" on the right side. Press.

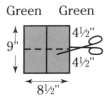

Green   Green

9"   4½"

4½"

8½"

Section 5 Piecing Diagram

Section 5 - Grass

Section 5 – Grass:

Refer to the Section 5 Piecing Diagram.

Sew 5 sets of 2 different Green 5" x 8½" strips together to make a
    5 pieces 8½" x 9".

Cut each piece into 2 strips 4½" x 8½".
    Make 10.

Scramble the patterns and sew 5 strips end to end to make a piece
    4½" x 40½". Press.
    Make 2.

Sew the 2 pieces together to make a row 8½" x 40½". Press.

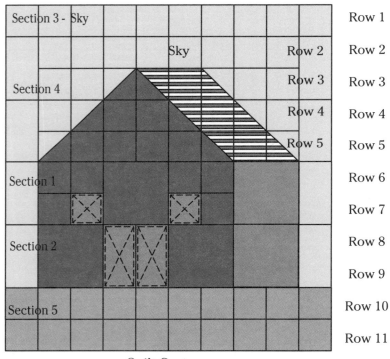

Section 3 - Sky								Row 1
			Sky			Row 2		Row 2
Section 4						Row 3		Row 3
						Row 4		Row 4
					Row 5			Row 5
Section 1								Row 6
								Row 7
Section 2								Row 8
								Row 9
Section 5								Row 10
								Row 11

Quilt Center

ASSEMBLY:
    Arrange all sections on a work surface or table.
    Refer to diagram for placement.
    Sew sections together. Press.

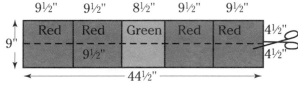

9½"   9½"   8½"   9½"   9½"

9"   Red   Red   Green   Red   Red   4½"

9½"   4½"

44½"

Pieced Border #1 Diagram
Sides

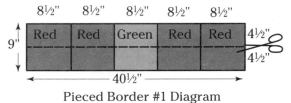

8½"   8½"   8½"   8½"   8½"

9"   Red   Red   Green   Red   Red   4½"

4½"

40½"

Pieced Border #1 Diagram
Top and Bottom

Barn - Quilt Assembly

Border #2:
Cut strips 2½" by the width of fabric.
Sew strips together end to end.
    Cut 2 strips 2½" x 52½" for sides.
    Cut 2 strips 2½" x 52½" for top and bottom.
    Sew side borders to the quilt. Press.
    Sew top and bottom borders to the quilt. Press.

Border #3:
Cut strips 4½" wide parallel to the selvage to
    eliminate piecing.
    Cut 2 strips 4½" x 56½" for sides.
    Cut 2 strips 4½" x 60½" for top and bottom.
    Sew side borders to the quilt. Press.
    Sew top and bottom borders to the quilt. Press.

FINISHING:
Appliques:
    See Basic Instructions.
    Sew scraps together to make pieces for the rooster,
        this adds to the charm of your rooster.
    Cut out pieces using patterns.
    Applique as desired.
    Cut out one of the circles from outer border fabric.
    Applique to a Green square and then to the barn
        as a hex sign.
Quilting: See Basic Instructions.
Binding: Cut strips 2½" wide.
    Sew together end to end to equal 258".
    See Binding Instructions.

Embroider marks across the windows and doors with a
    long and short Running stitch.
Embroider a French Knot or sew a button for the eye .

BORDERS:
Pieced Border #1:
Sides:
    Cut Red rectangles 9" x 9½".
    Sew together Red-Red-Green-Red-Red to make a
        piece 9" x 44½". Press.
    Cut the piece into 2 strips 4½" x 44½".
    Sew side borders to the quilt. Press.

Top and Bottom:
    Cut 4 Red rectangles 8½" x 9".
    Sew together Red-Red-Green-Red-Red to make a
        piece 9" x 40½". Press.
    Cut the piece into 2 strips 4½" x 40½".
    Sew a Green cornerstone to each end of each strip.
        Press.
    Sew top and bottom borders to the quilt. Press.

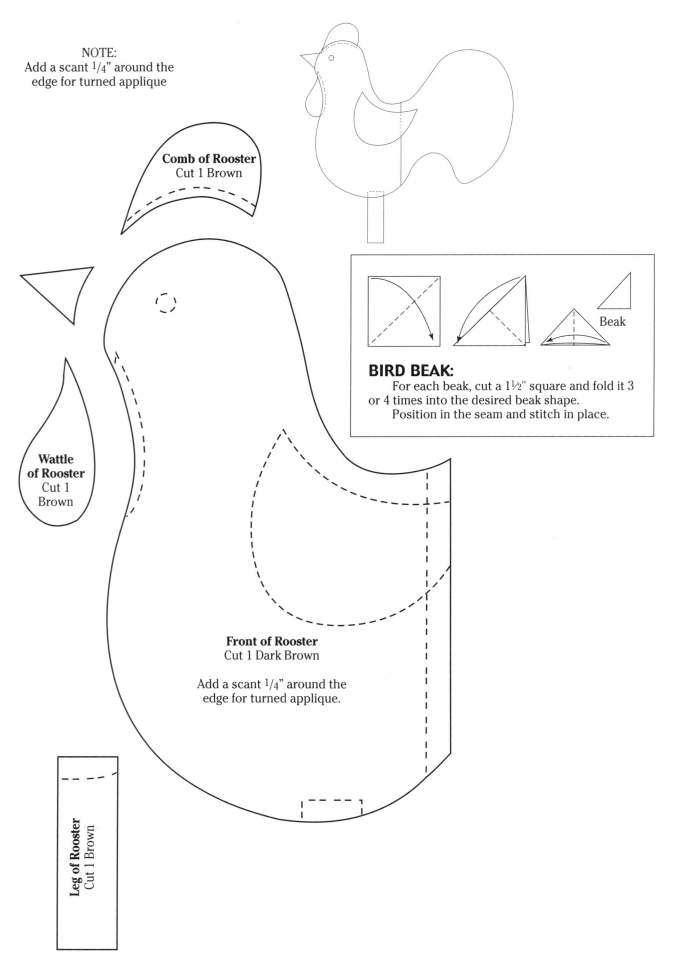

NOTE:
Add a scant ¼" around the
edge for turned applique

Comb of Rooster
Cut 1 Brown

**Wattle
of Rooster**
Cut 1
Brown

Beak

BIRD BEAK:
For each beak, cut a 1½" square and fold it 3
or 4 times into the desired beak shape.
Position in the seam and stitch in place.

Front of Rooster
Cut 1 Dark Brown

Add a scant ¼" around the
edge for turned applique.

Leg of Rooster
Cut 1 Brown

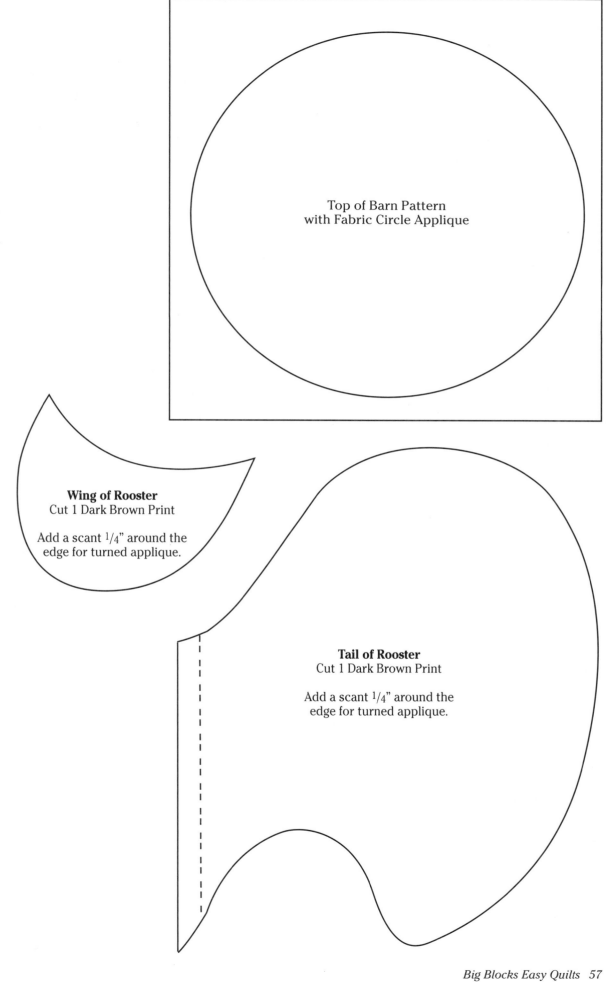

Top of Barn Pattern
with Fabric Circle Applique

Wing of Rooster
Cut 1 Dark Brown Print

Add a scant 1/4" around the
edge for turned applique.

Tail of Rooster
Cut 1 Dark Brown Print

Add a scant 1/4" around the
edge for turned applique.

Birds in the Garden

photo on page 13

SIZE: 56" x 64"

YARDAGE:

Yardage is given for using either fabric yardage or 'Layer Cake' squares.

We used a *Moda* "Louisa" by Terry Clothier Thompson 'Layer Cake' collection of 10" x 10" fabric squares - we purchased 1 'Layer Cake'

7 squares	OR	⅝ yard Red
3 squares	OR	⅓ yard Light Blue
4 squares	OR	⅓ yard Tan
1 square	OR	⅓ yard Dark Blue print
9 squares	OR	⅞ yard Green
8 squares	OR	⅝ yard Brown

Center & Border #7	Purchase ½ yard Brown
Borders #4, 8 & Binding	Purchase 1⅞ yards Tan
Backing	Purchase 3¼ yards
Batting	Purchase 64" x 72"

APPLIQUE FABRICS:

Birds & Small flower centers	Purchase ¼ yard Dark Blue or two 9" x 9" scraps
Bird beaks	Purchase ⅛ yard Yellow or 1½" x 3" scrap

Sewing machine, needle, thread

¼" buttons (2 Tan, 1 Black) for eyes

PREPARATION FOR SQUARES:

Cut all squares 10" x 10".

Label the stacks or pieces as you cut.

SORTING:

Sort the following 10" x 10" squares into stacks:

POSITION	QUANTITY & COLOR
Border 1	2 Red
Piano Key Border 2	1 Dark Blue, 3 Light Blue, 3 Tan
Border 3	4 Red
Border 5	7 Green, 8 Brown
Applique	1 Red, 1 Tan, 1 Green

CUTTING:

Cut a Center square 16½" x 16½".

Cut 12 Green and 10 Brown squares 4½" x 4½". Set aside for Border #6.

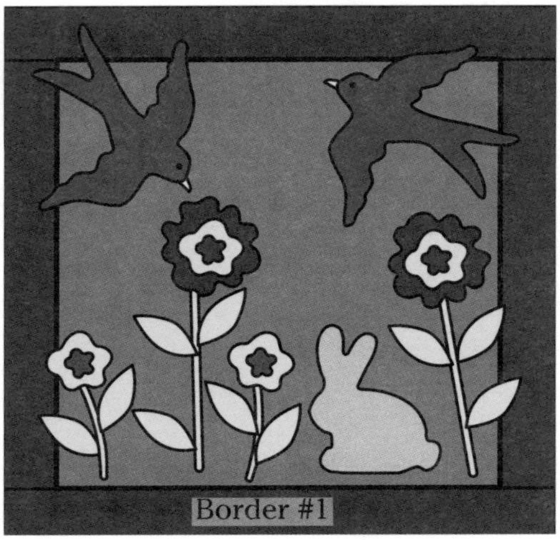

Applique Placement Diagram

BORDERS:

Red Border #1:

Cut 2 Red squares into strips 2½" x 10".

Sew strips together end to end.

Cut 2 strips 2½" x 16½" for sides.

Cut 2 strips 2½" x 20½" for top and bottom.

Sew side borders to the center block. Press.

Sew top and bottom borders to the center block. Press.

APPLIQUE:

See Basic Applique Instructions.

Applique birds, bunny and flowers as desired.

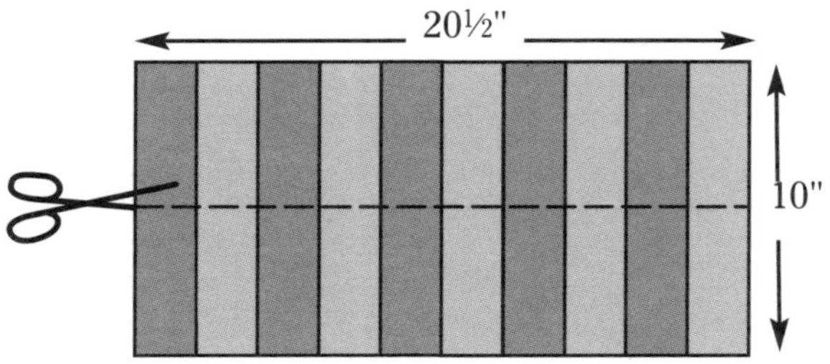

Piano Key Border Diagram

Piano Key Border #2:

Cut 1 Dark Blue square into 4 cornerstones 5" x 5".

From 3 Light Blue and 3 Tan squares, cut 10 Light Blue and 10 Tan 2½" x 10" strips.

Side Borders:

Use 5 strips of Tan and 5 strips of Blue.

Alternating the colors, Tan-Blue-Tan Blue, sew the strips together to make a piece 10" x 20½". Press.

Cut the strip into 2 sections 5" x 20½".

Sew side borders to the quilt. Press.

Top and Bottom Borders:

Use 5 strips of Tan and 5 strips of Blue.

Alternating the colors, Tan-Blue-Tan Blue, sew the strips together to make a piece 10" x 20½".

Cut the strip into 2 sections 5" x 20½".

Sew a Dark Blue cornerstone to each end. Press.

Sew top and bottom borders to the quilt. Press.

Red Pieced Border #3:

Cut 4 Red squares into strips 2½" x 10".
Sew strips together end to end.
> Cut 2 strips 2½" x 29½" for sides.
> Cut 2 strips 2½" x 33½" for top and bottom.
> Sew side borders to the quilt. Press.
> Sew top and bottom borders to the quilt. Press.

Tan Pieced Border #4:

Cut strips 2" x the width of fabric.
Sew strips together end to end.
> Cut 2 strips 2" x 33½" for sides.
> Cut 2 strips 2" x 36½" for top and bottom.
> Sew side borders to the quilt. Press.
> Sew top and bottom borders to the quilt. Press.

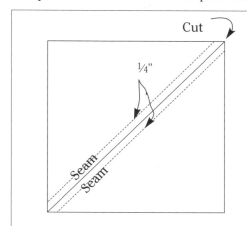

Half-Square Triangle Diagram

1. Place 2 squares right sides together.
2. Draw a diagonal line from corner to corner.
3. Stitch ¼" on each side of the line.
4. Cut squares apart on the diagonal line.
5. Open the 2 new squares with 2 colors.
6. Press. Trim off dog-ears.
7. Center and trim to size.

HALF-SQUARE TRIANGLES:

From 4 Green and 4 Brown squares cut 18 Brown and
18 Green 5" x 5" squares.
Match 18 pairs of Green - Brown for half-square triangles,:
Follow the instructions in the Half-Square Triangle
Diagram to make 36 half-square triangles.
Trim to 4½" x 4½".

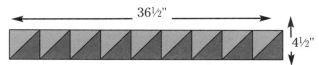

Half-Square Triangle Strip Diagram
Make 4
Two strips will be used as the side borders.

Half-Square Triangle Border #5:

Refer to Half-Square Triangle Strip diagram for block
placement and direction.
Sew 4 strips of 9 half-square triangles to make a piece
4½" x 36½". Press.

Side Borders -

Sew a strip to the right and left sides of the quilt. Press.

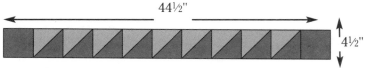

Half-Square Triangle - Top & Bottom Border Strips
Make 2

Top and Bottom Borders -

Cut 4 Brown cornerstone squares, each 4½" x 4½".
Sew a 4½" Brown square to each end of the remaining 2 strips.
Sew a strip to the top and bottom of the quilt. Press.

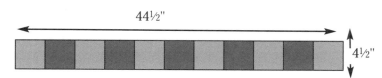

Border 6
Top & Bottom Checkerboard Strip Diagram
Make 2

Top and Bottom Checkerboard Borders #6 -

Refer to the Border 5 Top & Bottom Checkerboard Strip Diagram
Alternating Green and Brown, sew 11 squares together to
make a strip 4½" x 44½". Press. Make 2.
Sew a Checkerboard strip to the top and bottom of the quilt.
Press.

Birds in the Garden - Quilt Assembly Diagram

Border #7:

Cut strips 2½" by the width of fabric.
  Sew strips together end to end.
  Cut 2 strips 2½" x 52½" for sides.
  Cut 2 strips 2½" x 48½" for top
    and bottom.
  Sew side borders to the quilt.
    Press.
  Sew top and bottom borders to
    the quilt. Press.

Outer Border #8:

Cut strips 4½" wide parallel to the
    selvage to eliminate piecing.
  Cut 2 strips 4½" x 56½" for sides.
  Cut 2 strips 4½" x 56½" for top
    and bottom.
  Sew side borders to the quilt.
    Press.
  Sew top and bottom borders to
    the quilt. Press.

FINISHING:
Quilting: See Basic Instructions.
Binding:
Cut strips 2½" wide.
Sew together end to end to equal 250".
See Binding Instructions.

Birds in the Garden - Quilt Assembly Diagram

Bunny Rabbit
Cut 1 Tan

Add a scant ¹/₄" around the edge
for turned applique.

BIRD BEAK:

For each beak, cut a Yellow 1½" square and
fold it 3 or 4 times into the desired beak shape.
Position in the seam and stitch in place.

Beak

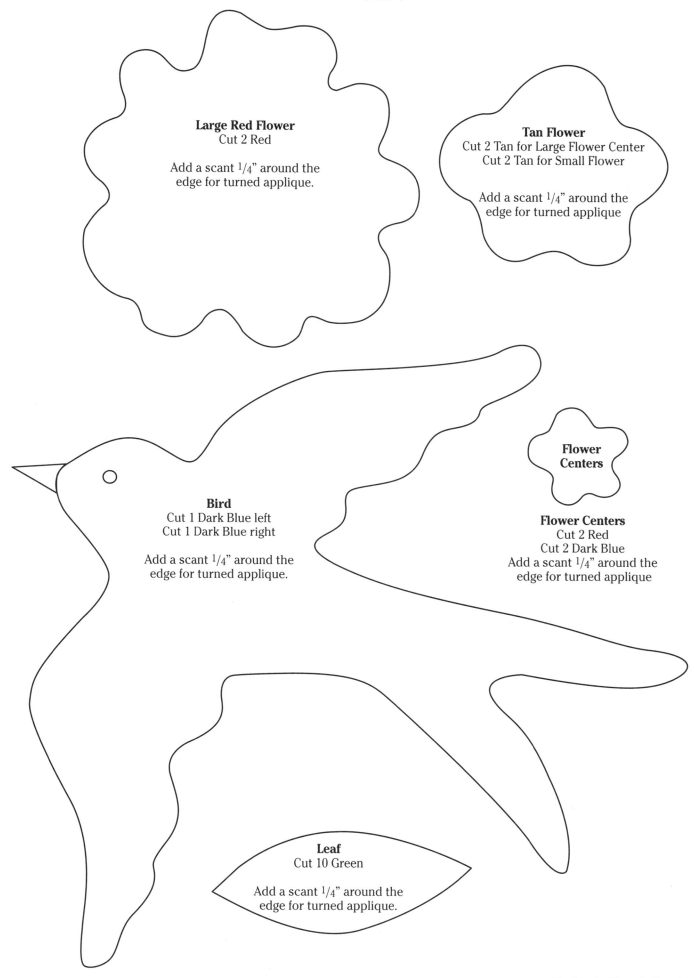

Large Red Flower
Cut 2 Red

Add a scant $1/4$" around the edge for turned applique.

Tan Flower
Cut 2 Tan for Large Flower Center
Cut 2 Tan for Small Flower

Add a scant $1/4$" around the edge for turned applique

Flower Centers

Flower Centers
Cut 2 Red
Cut 2 Dark Blue
Add a scant $1/4$" around the edge for turned applique

Bird
Cut 1 Dark Blue left
Cut 1 Dark Blue right

Add a scant $1/4$" around the edge for turned applique.

Leaf
Cut 10 Green

Add a scant $1/4$" around the edge for turned applique.

Blooms in the Garden

photo is on page 14

SIZE: 78" x 88"
TIP: Add more borders to make a larger quilt.

YARDAGE:
Yardage is given for using either fabric yardage or
   'Layer Cake' squares.
We used a *Moda* "Woodland Bloom" by Lila Tueller
   'Layer Cake' collection of 10" x 10" fabric squares
   - we purchased 1 'Layer Cake'

8 squares	OR	⅝ yard Pink
6 squares	OR	⅝ yard Green
5 squares	OR	⅝ yard Tan
4 squares	OR	⅓ yard White
4 squares	OR	⅓ yard Turquoise
4 squares	OR	⅓ yard Brown
2 squares	OR	⅓ yard Rust
2 squares	OR	⅓ yard Aqua
1 square	OR	⅓ yard Red

Border #2, E, H, & I	Purchase 1 yard Red
Border #1 & #3, F, G, & Sashing	Purchase 1⅞ yards Green
Border #4 & Binding	Purchase 2¼ yards Turquoise
Backing	Purchase 5⅔ yards
Batting	Purchase 86" x 96"
Sewing machine, needle, thread	

PREPARATION FOR SQUARES:
   Cut all squares 10" x 10".
   Label the stacks or pieces as you cut.

SORTING:
   Sort the following 10" x 10" squares into stacks:

POSITION	QUANTITY & COLOR
Block 1:	4 Tan for A, B, C, & D
Block 2:	1 Aqua for A, 1 Red for B, 2 Rust for C & D
Block 3:	4 White for A, B, C, & D
Block 4:	1 Aqua for A, 2 Green for B & D, 1 Tan for C
Block 5:	4 Turquoise for A, B, C, & D
Block 6:	4 Pink for A, B, C, & D
Block 7:	4 Brown for A, B, C, & D
Block 8:	4 Pink for A, B, C, & D
Block 9:	4 Green for A, B, C, & D

CUT THESE STRIPS FROM YARDAGE:
Cut 36 Red 4" x 4" squares for E.
Cut 108 Green 3" x 3" squares for F.
Cut 36 Green 1½" x 6¼" Sashing strips for G.
Cut 36 Red 1½" x 4¼" Sashing strips for H.
Cut 9 Red 1½" x 1½" squares for I.
Cut 6 Green 1½" x 20½" horizontal sashing strips for J.

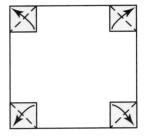
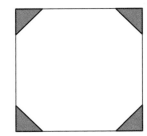

SNOWBALL UNITS:
Units A, B, C, and D are constructed in the same manner.
The only variation is the position of the Red corner of the snowball.
   Refer to the Block Assembly Diagram for placement.
   Align 1 Red and 3 Green squares in the corners as shown.
   Draw a diagonal line as shown. Sew on the line and fold back the triangle. Press.
   Repeat for all corners.
   Make 4 for each block, a total of 36.

SASHING STRIPS:
   Sew G-H end to end to make a piece 1½" x 10". Press.
   Make 36.

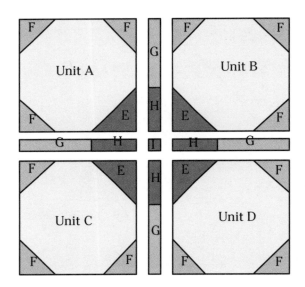

BLOCK ASSEMBLY:
Row 1: Sew Unit A -Sashing G-H -Unit B. Press.
Row 2: Sew G/H - I - H/G. Press.
Row 3: Sew Unit C -Sashing G-H -Unit D. Press.
   Sew the rows together. Press.

   The block will measure 20½" x 20½" at this point.
   Make 9 blocks.

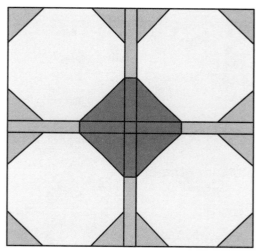

Assembled Block - Make 9
The block will measure 20½" x 20½" at this point.

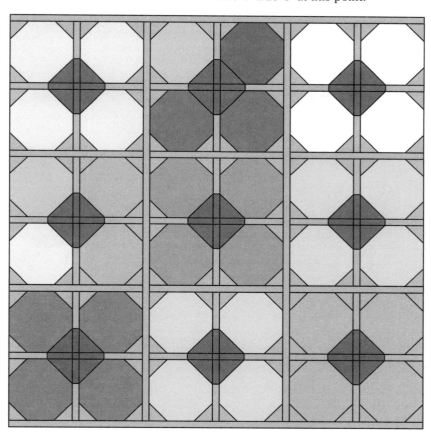

Blooms in the Garden - Quilt Assembly

COLUMN ASSEMBLY:
Column 1: Sew Block 1- J- Block 4- J- Block 7. Press.
Column 2: Sew Block 2- J- Block 5- J- Block 8. Press.
Column 3: Sew Block 3- J- Block 6- J- Block 9. Press.

GREEN VERTICAL SASHING:
Cut 3 Green strips 1½" x width of fabric.
Sew strips end to end. Press.
    Cut 2 strips 1½" x 62½".
    Sew:
Column 1-Sashing-Column 2-Sashing-Column 3.
Press.

BORDERS:
Top and Bottom Green Border #1:
Cut 3 Green strips 1½" x width of fabric.
Sew strips end to end. Press.
    Cut 2 strips 1½" x 62½" for the
      top and bottom.
    Sew top and bottom borders to the
      quilt. Press.

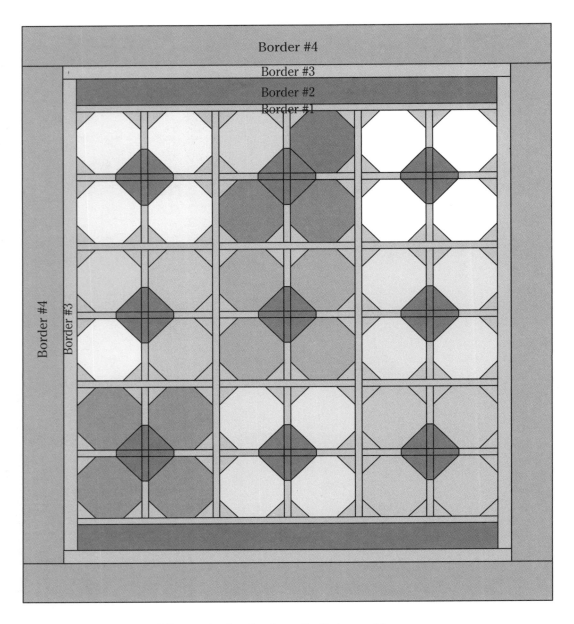

Blooms in the Garden - Quilt Assembly

Red Border #2:
Cut 3 Red strips 4½" x width of fabric.
Sew strips end to end. Press.
   Cut 2 strips 4½" x 62½" for the top and bottom.
   Sew top and bottom borders to the quilt. Press.

Border #3:
Cut strips 2½" by the width of fabric.
Sew strips together end to end.
   Cut 2 strips 2½" x 72½" for sides.
   Cut 2 strips 2½" x 66½" for top and bottom.
   Sew side borders to the quilt. Press.
   Sew top and bottom borders to the quilt. Press.

Border #4:
Cut strips 6½" wide parallel to the selvage to
     eliminate piecing.
   Cut 2 strips 6½" x 76½" for sides.
   Cut 2 strips 6½" x 78½" for top and bottom.
   Sew side borders to the quilt. Press.
   Sew top and bottom borders to the quilt. Press.

FINISHING:
Quilting: See Basic Instructions.
Binding: Cut strips 2½" wide.
     Sew together end to end to equal 342".
     See Binding Instructions.

Square by Square

photo is on page 15

SIZE: 70" x 79"

YARDAGE:
Yardage is given for using either fabric yardage or 10" squares.
We used a *Moda* "Heritage" by Howard Marcus
  'Layer Cake' collection of 10" x 10" fabric squares
  - we purchased 1 'Layer Cake'

13 squares	OR	1⅙ yards Tan
3 squares	OR	⅓ yard Blue Green
9 squares	OR	⅞ yard Medium Brown
2 squares	OR	⅓ yard Red
7 squares	OR	⅝ yard Dark Brown

Center panel	Purchase 1 yard Tan print
Border #3	Purchase ½ yard Chocolate Brown
Border #4 & Binding	Purchase 2 yards Brown print
Backing	Purchase 5½ yards
Batting	Purchase 78" x 87"

Sewing machine, needle, thread

SORTING: Sort the following 10" x 10" squares into stacks:

POSITION	QUANTITY & COLOR
Half-square triangle cornerstones	2 Red, 2 Med. Brown
Pieced Border #1	4 Dark Brown
Pieced Border #2	13 Tan, 3 Blue-Green, 3 Dark Brown, 7 Med. Brown

CUTTING:
Cut a Tan print Center panel 23½" x 32½":

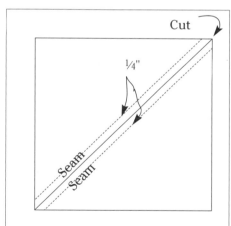

Half-Square Triangle Diagram
1. Place 2 squares right sides together.
2. Draw a diagonal line from corner to corner.
3. Stitch ¼" on each side of the line.
4. Cut squares apart on the diagonal line.
5. Open the 2 new squares with 2 colors.
6. Press. Trim off dog-ears.
7. Center and trim to size.

HALF-SQUARE TRIANGLES:
  Match the following squares for the half-square triangles:
  2 pairs of Red Medium Brown

  Follow the instructions in the Half-Square Triangle Diagram to make 4 half-square triangles.
  Trim to 9½" x 9½".

BORDERS:
Pieced Border #1:
  From 4 Dark Brown squares cut 13 strips 2½" x 10".
  Sew the strips end to end.
    Cut 2 strips 2½" x 32½" for sides.
    Cut 2 strips 2½" x 27½" for top and bottom.
  Sew side borders to the Center Panel. Press.
  Sew top and bottom borders to the Panel. Press.

Square by Square - Quilt Assembly Diagram

PREPARATION FOR PIECED BORDER #2:
  Cut all squares 5" x 5".
  Label the stacks of colors or pieces as you cut.

Pieced Border #2:
  Arrange all blocks on a work surface or table.
  Refer to the Quilt Assembly diagram for block placement.
  Sew the sections together. Press.
    Sew side borders to the quilt. Press.
    Sew top and bottom borders to the quilt. Press.

Border #3:
  Cut strips 2½" by the width of fabric.
  Sew strips together end to end.
    Cut 2 strips 2½" x 63½" for sides.
    Cut 2 strips 2½" x 58½" for top and bottom.
  Sew side borders to the quilt. Press.
  Sew top and bottom borders to the quilt. Press.

Outer Border #4:
Cut strips 6½" wide parallel to the selvage to eliminate piecing.
    Cut 2 strips 6½" x 67½" for sides.
    Cut 2 strips 6½" x 70½" for top and bottom.
  Sew side borders to the quilt. Press.
  Sew top and bottom borders to the quilt. Press.

FINISHING:
Quilting: See Basic Instructions.
Binding: Cut strips 2½" wide.
    Sew together end to end to equal 308".
    See Binding Instructions.

Pretty in Pink

photo is on page 15

SIZE: 56" x 69½"

TIP: Add more borders to make a larger quilt.

YARDAGE:

Yardage is given for using either fabric yardage or 10" squares.
We used a *Moda* "Charisma" by Chez Moi
    'Layer Cake' collection of 10" x 10" fabric squares
    - we purchased 1 'Layer Cake'

6 squares	OR	⅝ yard Pink-Red print
4 squares	OR	⅓ yard Pink
4 squares	OR	⅓ yard Red
2 squares	OR	⅓ yard Brown
1 square	OR	⅓ yard Gold
1 square	OR	⅓ yard Stripe
1 square	OR	⅓ yard Ivory
1 square	OR	⅓ yard Blue

Sashings B, C, D, E   Purchase 1⅛ yards Pink
Border #1 & Binding   Purchase 1¾ yards Pink-Red print
Backing   Purchase 4 yards
Batting   Purchase 64" x 78"

Sewing machine, needle, thread
DMC pearl cotton or 6-ply floss
#22 or #24 chenille needle

PREPARATION FOR SQUARES:
    Cut all squares 10" x 10".
    Label the squares as you sort.

SORTING:
    Choose twenty 10" x 10" squares for blocks:

POSITION	QUANTITY & COLOR
Blocks 7, 9, 10, 12, 17, 20	6 Pink-Red prints
Blocks 1, 2, 8, 19	4 Pink
Blocks 3, 6, 13, 18	4 Red
Blocks 5, 15	2 Brown
Block 14	1 Gold
Block 11	1 Stripe
Block 16	1 Ivory

SASH CUTTING:

Cut 20 of Strip B	2½" x 10".
Cut 20 of Strip C	2½" x 12".
Cut 1 of Strip D	2½" x 58".
Cut 2 of Strip E	2½" x 48½".

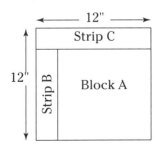

Odd-Numbered Blocks - Make 10

SEW BLOCKS:
    Sew a Strip B to the left side of every Block A. Press.
    Refer to the Block Assembly Diagrams.

Odd Numbered Blocks:
    For odd numbered blocks, sew Strip C to the top. Press.

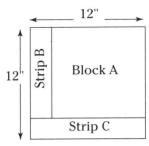

Even-Numbered Blocks
Make 10

Even Numbered Blocks:
    For even numbered blocks, sew Strip C to the bottom. Press.
    Each block will measure 12" x 12" at this point.

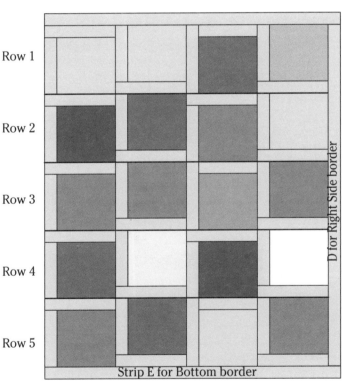

ASSEMBLY:
    Arrange all blocks on a work surface or table.
    Refer to diagram for block placement and direction.
    Sew blocks together in 5 rows, 4 blocks per row. Press.
    Sew rows together. Press.
    Strip D border - Sew to the right side of the quilt. Press.
    Strip E border - Sew to the top and bottom of quilt. Press.

BORDER:
Outside Border:
Cut strips 4½" wide parallel to the selvage to eliminate piecing.
    Cut 2 strips 4½" x 62" for sides.
    Cut 2 strips 4½" x 56½" for top and bottom.
    Sew side borders to the quilt. Press.
    Sew top and bottom borders to the quilt. Press.

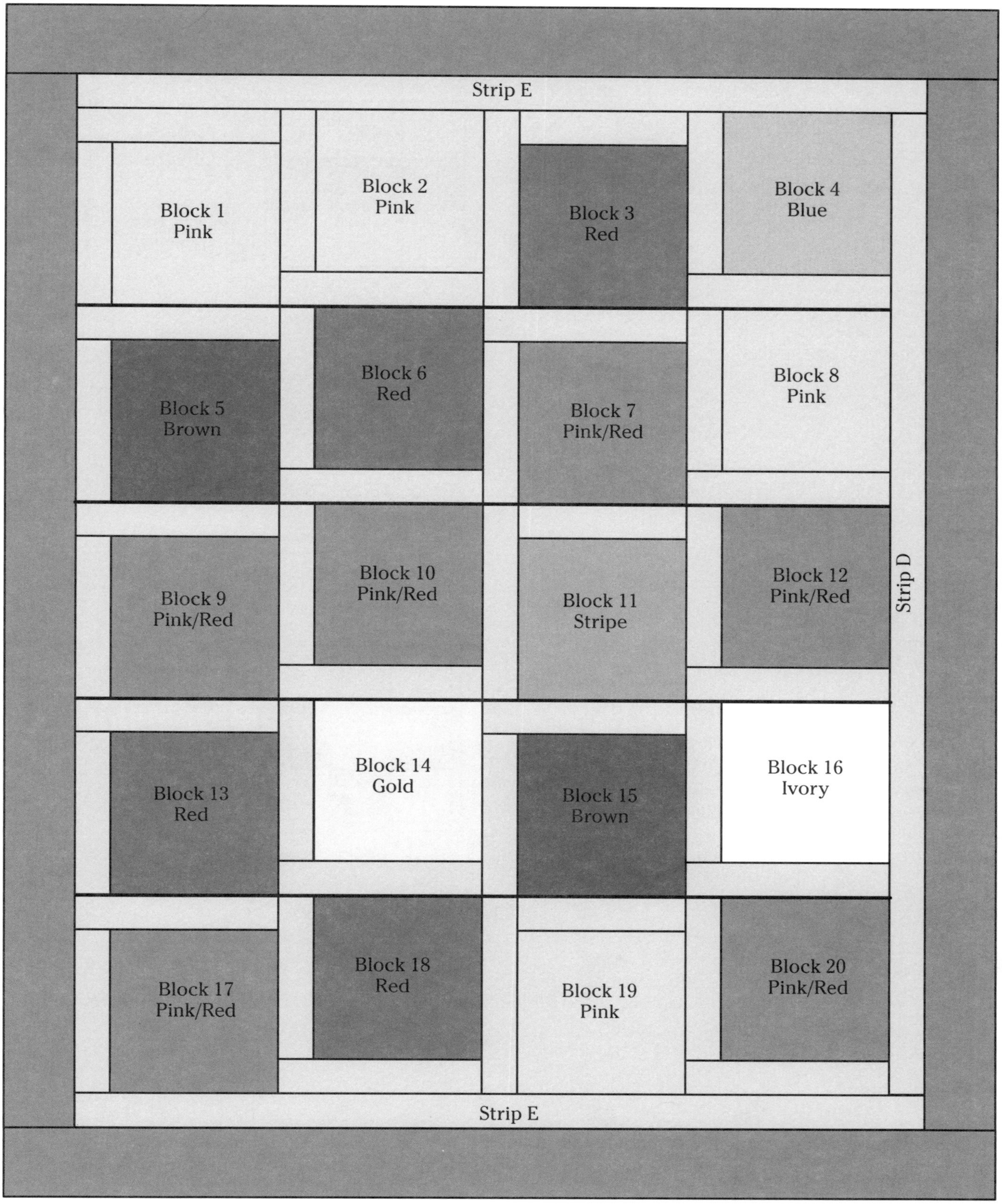

Strip E

| Block 1 Pink | Block 2 Pink | Block 3 Red | Block 4 Blue |

| Block 5 Brown | Block 6 Red | Block 7 Pink/Red | Block 8 Pink |

| Block 9 Pink/Red | Block 10 Pink/Red | Block 11 Stripe | Block 12 Pink/Red |

| Block 13 Red | Block 14 Gold | Block 15 Brown | Block 16 Ivory |

| Block 17 Pink/Red | Block 18 Red | Block 19 Pink | Block 20 Pink/Red |

Strip D

Strip E

Pretty in Pink
Quilt Assembly Diagram

APPLIQUE:
Cut pleasing shapes from print border fabric.
Refer to the Basic Instructions.
Applique as desired. We placed appliques in
Blocks 2, 3, 5, 14, 16, and 18.

FINISHING:
Quilting: See Basic Instructions.
Binding: Cut strips 2½" wide.
Sew together end to end to equal 261".
See Binding Instructions.

Star Crossed

photo is on pages 16 - 17

SIZE: 66" x 79"
TIP: Add more borders to make a larger quilt.

YARDAGE:
Yardage is given for using either fabric yardage or
   'Layer Cake' squares.
We used a *Moda* "Pine Creek Crossing" by Holly Taylor
   'Layer Cake' collection of 10" x 10" fabric squares
   - we purchased 2 'Layer Cakes'

13 squares	OR	1⅙ yards Black
22 squares	OR	1¾ yards Tan
7 squares	OR	⅝ yard Cream
8 squares	OR	⅝ yard Green

Border #2 & Sashing	Purchase ⅔ yard Black print
Border #3 & Binding	Purchase 2 yards Green
Backing	Purchase 5⅛ yards
Batting	Purchase 75" x 88"

Sewing machine, needle, thread

PREPARATION FOR SQUARES:
   Cut all squares 10" x 10".
   Label the stacks or pieces as you cut.

SORTING:
   Sort the following 10" x 10" squares into stacks:

POSITION	QUANTITY & COLOR
Snowballs	13 Tan, 6 Black
Checkerboards	7 Cream, 6 Black
Cornerstones	1 Black
Piano Keys	8 Green, 9 Tan

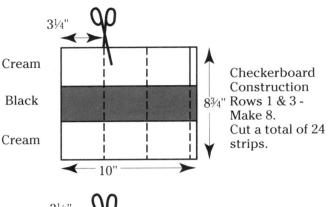

3¼"

Cream

Black

Cream

8¾"

10"

Checkerboard
Construction
Rows 1 & 3 -
Make 8.
Cut a total of 24
strips.

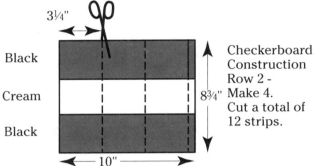

3¼"

Black

Cream

Black

8¾"

10"

Checkerboard
Construction
Row 2 -
Make 4.
Cut a total of
12 strips.

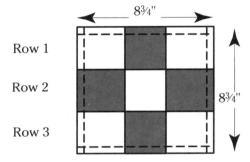

8¾"

Row 1

Row 2

Row 3

8¾"

Checkerboard Block - Make 12.

 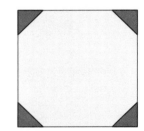

Snowball Corners Diagram - Make 13

SNOWBALL BLOCKS:
   Cut 13 Tan squares 8¾" x 8¾".
   Cut 52 Black squares 3¼" x 3¼".
   Refer to the Snowball Corners diagram.
   For each block, align a 3¼" square with each corner.
   Draw a diagonal line as shown and sew on the line.
   Fold the corner back and press.
   Repeat for all corners.

.CHECKERBOARD BLOCKS:
   You will need 7 Cream and 6 Black 10" squares.
   Cut 20 Cream strips 3¼" x 10".
   Cut 16 Black strips 3¼" x 10".
   Refer to the Checkerboard Construction diagrams.

   Make 8 sets of Cream-Black-Cream.
   Make 4 sets of Black-Cream-Black.
   Sew each set together to make a piece 8¾" x 10".
   Press.
   Cut each set into strips 3¼" x 8¾".

   You need:

Rows 1 & 3	24 Cream-Black-Cream strips
Row 2's	12 Black-Cream-Black strips

   Refer to the Checkerboard Block diagram.
   Arrange 3 rows for each block.
   Sew the rows together. Press.
   Each block will measure 8¾" x 8¾" at this point.

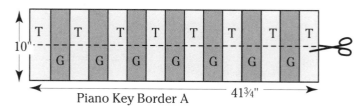

Piano Key Border A   41¾"

Piano Key Border #1:
> You need 8 Green and 9 Tan 10" squares.
> Cut each square into 3 strips 3¼" x 10".

Border A (Inner Top & Bottom Borders):
> You need 8 Tan and 7 Green strips.
> Sew Tan-Green-Tan-Green etc, ending in a Tan. Press.
> The strip-set will measure 10" x 41¾" at this point.
> Cut the strip-set into 2 strips 5" x 41¾". (Borders A)

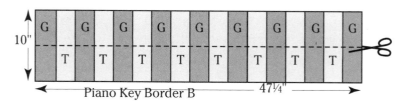

Piano Key Border B   47¼"

Border B (Side Borders):
> You need 9 Green and 10 Tan strips.
> Cut 2 Tan strips to 2¼" x 10". Set these aside.
> Using 8 Tan and 9 Green, sew Green-Tan-Green-Tan etc,
>   ending in a Green. Press.
> The piece will measure 10" x 47¼" at this point.
> Sew a Tan 2¼" x 10" to each end of the strip-set. Press.
> Cut the strip-set into 2 strips 5" x 50¾" (Borders B).

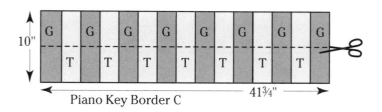

Piano Key Border C   41¾"

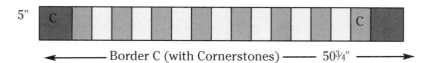

Border C (with Cornerstones) ———— 50¾"

Border C (Outer Top & Bottom Borders):
> You need 8 Green and 7 Tan strips.
> Sew Green-Tan-Green-Tan etc, ending in a Green. Press.
> The strip-set will measure 10" x 41¾" at this point.
> Cut the strip-set into 2 strips 5" x 41¾" (Borders C).

Black Cornerstones:
> Cut 4 Black Cornerstones 5" x 5".
> Sew one to each end of both Border C's. Press.
> The strip-set will measure 5" x 50¾" at this point (Border C)

2½"

Black Sashing - Make 2   50¾"

Black Sashing D:
> Cut 3 Black border strips 2½" by the width of fabric.
> Sew strips together end to end. Press. Cut 2 strips 2½" x 50¾".

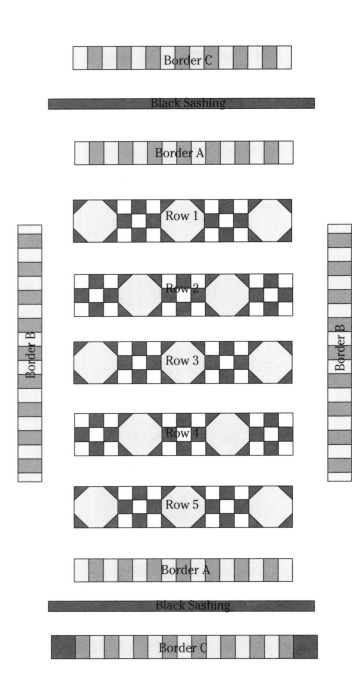

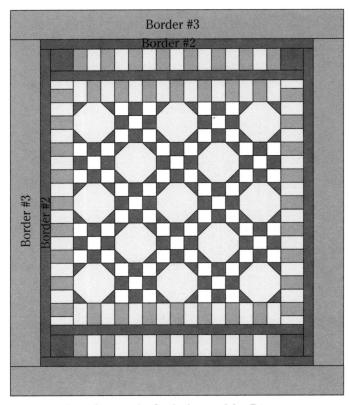

Star Crossed - Quilt Assembly Diagram

ASSEMBLY:
Arrange all blocks on a work surface or table.
Refer to Quilt Assembly diagram for block placement.
Sew blocks together in 5 rows, 5 blocks per row. Press.
Sew rows together. Press.

Sew Borders to the Quilt:
Sew a Border A to the top and bottom of the quilt. Press.
Sew a Border B to each side of the quilt. Press.
Sew a strip of Black Sashing to the
    top and bottom of the quilt. Press.

Sew a Black Cornerstone to each end of Border C. Press.
Sew a Border C to the top and bottom of the quilt. Press.

BORDERS:
Border #2:
Cut strips 2½" by the width of fabric.
Sew strips together end to end.
    Cut 2 strips 2½" x 63¾" for sides.
    Cut 2 strips 2½" x 54¾" for top and bottom.
    Sew side borders to the quilt. Press.
    Sew top and bottom borders to the quilt. Press.

Outer Border #3:
Cut strips 6½" wide parallel to the selvage to
        eliminate piecing.
    Cut 2 strips 6½" x 67¾" for sides.
    Cut 2 strips 6½" x 66¾" for top and bottom.
    Sew side borders to the quilt. Press.
    Sew top and bottom borders to the quilt. Press.

FINISHING:
Quilting:
    See Basic Instructions.
Binding:
    Cut strips 2½" wide.
    Sew together end to end to equal 301".
    See Binding Instructions.

Note: This quilt is also available in a pattern pack
        #0961 "Star Crossed" by Design Originals.

Star Crossed Pillow

pieced by Lanelle Herron

Use leftover fabrics to make this fabulous complement for your Star-Crossed quilt. It also makes a lovely stand-alone small project.

Remember this one next time you need a quick birthday or Father's Day gift.

SIZE: 17¾" x 17¾"

YARDAGE:

We used a *Moda* "Pine Creek Crossing" by Holly Taylor 'Layer Cake' collection of 10" x 10" fabric squares
- we used leftover squares from Star Crossed Quilt

2 squares	OR	⅓ yard Black
1 square	OR	⅓ yard Tan
1 square	OR	⅓ yard Cream

Border & Backing   Purchase ⅔ yard Green print
Pillow form   Purchase a 14" x 14"
Sewing machine, needle, thread

SORTING:
Sort the following 10" x 10" squares into stacks:

POSITION	QUANTITY AND COLOR
Center	1 Tan, 1 Black
Border	1 Cream, 1 Black

CUTTING:
Cut 1 Tan square 8¾" x 8¾" for Center block.
Cut 2 Black strips 3¼" x 10" for Checkerboard border.
Cut 2 Cream strips 3¼" x 10" for Checkerboard border.
Cut 2 Cream squares 3¼" x 3¼" for Checkerboard side borders.
Cut 2 Black squares 3¼" x 3¼" for Checkerboard top and bottom borders.
Cut 4 Black squares 3¼" x 3¼" for Snowball corners.

 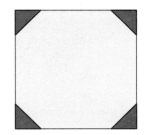

CENTER BLOCK:
Refer to the Snowball Corners diagram.
Align a square with each corner.
Draw a diagonal line as shown and sew on the line.
Fold the corner back and press. Repeat for all corners.

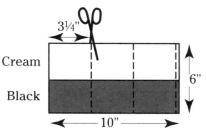

Checkerboard Construction
Make 2.
Cut a total of 6 strips.

CHECKERBOARD BORDER:
Checkerboard Border #1:
Refer to the Checkerboard Construction diagrams.
Make 2 sets of Black-Cream strips.
Sew each set together to make a piece 6" x 10". Press.
Cut each set into 3 strips 3¼" x 6".
Sides: Sew a Cream square to a Black-Cream strip. Press. Make 2. Sew to the sides of the Snowball block.
Top and Bottom: Sew 2 Black-Cream strips end to end. Sew a Black square to the end. Press. Make 2. Sew a strip to the top and bottom of the pillow. Press.

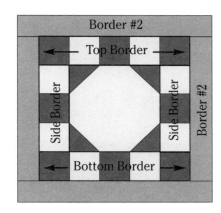

Star Crossed Pillow - Assembly Diagram

PILLOW BORDER:
Border #2:
Cut 2 strips 2½" x 14¼" for sides.
Cut 2 strips 2½" x 18¼" for top and bottom.
Sew side borders to the pillow. Press.
Sew top and bottom borders to the pillow. Press.

PILLOW BACK:
Cut 2 backing pieces 17" x 18¼".
Press and sew a ¼" hem along one 18¼" edge of each backing piece.
Press a 5" hem along the same edge of each piece.
With right sides together, align the pillow back pieces with the edge of the pillow front. The hemmed edges will overlap near the center of the pillow.
Sew a ¼" seam all around the pillow. Press.
Turn the pillow right side out.

FINISHING:
Quilting:
Stitch in the ditch along the outer edge of Border #1.
Quilt the outer border as desired.

The Best Things About 'Layer Cakes'

I love to quilt, but it is often difficult to find time to cut and piece a quilt top. When I saw collections of 10" pre-cut squares, I knew they were the answer.

No more spending hours choosing and cutting fabrics. Now I can begin sewing right away. Beautiful colors are available in every set. So whether I like jewel colors, heritage patterns, soft pastels or earthy tones... there is an assortment for me.

Now my goals... a handmade cover for every bed, an heirloom quilt for each new baby and a pieced quilt for each of my children... are within reach. With 'Layer Cakes' it is possible to complete a quilt top in a weekend.

After I piece all the blocks together, I use leftover strips for the borders and binding. Nothing really goes to waste and, if needed, I can purchase a bit of extra fabric for an extra punch of color or an additional yard for the border.

TIP: Quantities are given in strips and yardage so you know what you need and can start right away.

Tips for Working with Squares

Guide for Yardage:

10" x 10" Squares - Four 10" squares can be cut from ⅓ yard or eight 10" squares can be cut from ⅝ yard.

These tips will help reduce stretching and make your quilt lay flat for quilting.

1. If you are cutting yardage, cut on the grain. Cut fat quarters on grain, parallel to the 18" side.

2. When sewing crosswise grain squares together, take care not to stretch the squares. If you detect any puckering as you go, rip out the seam and sew it again.

3. Press, Do Not Iron. Carefully open fabric, with the seam to one side, press without moving the iron. A back-and-forth ironing motion stretches the fabric.

4. Reduce the wiggle in your borders with this technique from garment making. First, accurately cut your borders to the exact measure of the quilt top. Then, before sewing the border to the quilt, run a double row of stay stitches along the outside edge to maintain the original shape and prevent stretching. Pin the border to the quilt, taking care not to stretch the quilt top to make it fit. Pinning reduces slipping and stretching.

Rotary Cutting

Rotary Cutter: Friend or Foe

A rotary cutter is wonderful and useful. When not used correctly, the sharp blade can be a dangerous tool. Follow these safety tips:

1. Never cut toward you.
2. Use a sharp blade. Pressing harder on a dull blade can cause the blade to jump the ruler and injure your fingers.
3. Always disengage the blade before the cutter leaves your hand, even if you intend to pick it up immediately.

Rotary cutters have been caught when lifting fabric, have fallen onto the floor and have cut fingers.

Basic Sewing

You now have precisely cut strips that are exactly the correct width. You are well on your way to blocks that fit together perfectly. Accurate sewing is the next important step.

Matching Edges:

1. Carefully line up the edges of your strips. Many times, if the underside is off a little, your seam will be off by $\frac{1}{8}$". This does not sound like much until you have 8 seams in a block, each off by $\frac{1}{8}$". Now your finished block is a whole inch wrong!

2. Pin the pieces together to prevent them shifting.

Seam Allowance:

I cannot stress enough the importance of accurate $\frac{1}{4}$" seams. All the quilts in this book are measured for $\frac{1}{4}$" seams unless otherwise indicated.

Most sewing machine manufacturers offer a Quarter-inch foot. A Quarter-inch foot is the most worthwhile investment you can make in your quilting.

Pressing:

I want to talk about pressing even before we get to sewing because proper pressing can make the difference between a quilt that wins a ribbon at the quilt show and one that does not.

Press, do NOT iron. What does that mean? Many of us want to move the iron back and forth along the seam. This "ironing" stretches the strip out of shape and creates errors that accumulate as the quilt is constructed. Believe it or not, there is a correct way to press your seams, and here it is:

1. Do NOT use steam with your iron. If you need a little water, spritz it on.

2. Place your fabric flat on the ironing board without opening the seam. Set a hot iron on the seam and count to 3. Lift the iron and move to the next position along the seam. Repeat until the entire seam is pressed. This sets and sinks the threads into the fabric.

3. Now, carefully lift the top strip and fold it away from you so the seam is on one side. Usually the seam is pressed toward the darker fabric, but often the direction of the seam is determined by the piecing requirements.

4. Press the seam open with your fingers. Add a little water or spray starch if it wants to close again. Lift the iron and place it on the seam. Count to 3. Lift the iron again and continue until the seam is pressed. Do NOT

use the tip of the iron to push the seam open. So many people do this and wonder later why their blocks are not fitting together.

5. Most critical of all: For accuracy every seam must be pressed before the next seam is sewn.

Working with 'Crosswise Grain' Strips:

Strips cut on the crosswise grain (from selvage to selvage) have problems similar to bias edges and are prone to stretching. To reduce stretching and make your quilt lay flat for quilting, keep these tips in mind.

1. Take care not to stretch the strips as you sew.

2. Adjust the sewing thread tension and the presser foot pressure if needed.

3. If you detect any puckering as you go, rip out the seam and sew it again. It is much easier to take out a seam now than to do it after the block is sewn.

Sewing Bias Edges:

Bias edges wiggle and stretch out of shape very easily. They are not recommended for beginners, but even a novice can accomplish bias edges if these techniques are employed.

1. Stabilize the bias edge with one of these methods:

    a) Press with spray starch.

    b) Press freezer paper or removable iron-on stabilizer to the back of the fabric.

    c) Sew a double row of stay stitches along the bias edge and $\frac{1}{8}$" from the bias edge. This is a favorite technique of garment makers.

2. Pin, pin, pin! I know many of us dislike pinning, but when working with bias edges, pinning makes the difference between intersections that match and those that do not.

Building Better Borders:

Wiggly borders make a quilt very difficult to finish. However, wiggly borders can be avoided with these techniques.

1. Cut the borders on grain. That means cutting your strips parallel to the selvage edge.

2. Accurately cut your borders to the exact measure of the quilt.

3. If your borders are piece stripped from crosswise grain fabrics, press well with spray starch and sew a double row of stay stitches along the outside edge to maintain the original shape and prevent stretching.

4. Pin the border to the quilt, taking care not to stretch the quilt top to make it fit. Pinning reduces slipping and stretching.

Embroidery Use 24" lengths of doubled pearl cotton or 6-ply floss and a #22 or #24 Chenille needle (this needle has a large eye). Outline large elements.

Running Stitch Come up at A. Weave the needle through the fabric, making LONG stitches on the top and SHORT stitches on the bottom. Keep stitches even.

Applique Instructions

Basic Turned Edge

1. Trace pattern onto no-melt template plastic (or onto Wash-Away Tear-Away Stabilizer).

2. Cut out the fabric shape leaving a scant ¼" fabric border all around and clip the curves.

3. **Plastic Template Method -** Place plastic shape on the wrong side of the fabric. Spray edges with starch. Press a¼" border over the edge of the template plastic with the tip of a hot iron. Press firmly.

   Stabilizer Method - Place stabilizer shape on the wrong side of the fabric. Use a glue stick to press a ¼" border over the edge of the stabilizer securing it with the glue stick. Press firmly.

5. Remove the template, maintaining the folded edge on the back of the fabric.

6. Position the shape on the quilt and Blindstitch in place.

Basic Turned Edge by Hand

1. Cut out the shape leaving a ¼" fabric border all around.

2. Baste the shapes to the quilt, keeping the basting stitches away from the edge of the fabric.

3. Begin with all areas that are under other layers and work to the topmost layer.

4. For an area no more than 2" ahead of where you are working, trim to ⅛" and clip the curves.

5. Using the needle, roll the edge under and sew tiny Blindstitches to secure.

Using Fusible Web for Iron-on Applique:

1. Trace pattern onto Steam a Seam 2 fusible web.

2. Press the patterns onto the wrong side of fabric.

3. Cut out patterns exactly on the drawn line.

4. Score web paper with a pin, then remove the paper.

5. Position the fabric, fusible side down, on the quilt. Press with a hot iron following the fusible web manufacturer's instructions.

6. Stitch around the edge by hand.

Optional: Stabilize the wrong side of the fabric with your favorite stabilizer.

   Use a size 80 machine embroidery needle. Fill the bobbin with lightweight basting thread and thread machine with machine embroidery thread that complements the color being appliqued.

   Set your machine for a Zigzag stitch and adjust the thread tension if needed. Use a scrap to experiment with different stitch widths and lengths until you find the one you like best.

   Sew slowly.

Basic Layering Instructions

Marking Your Quilt:

   If you choose to mark your quilt for hand or machine quilting, it is much easier to do so before layering. Press your quilt before you begin. Here are some handy tips regarding marking.

1. A disappearing pen may vanish before you finish.

2. Use a White pencil on dark fabrics.

3. If using a washable Blue pen, remember that pressing may make the pen permanent.

Pieced Backings:

1. Press the backing fabric before measuring.

2. If possible cut backing fabrics on grain, parallel to the selvage edges.

3. Piece 3 parts rather than 2 whenever possible, sewing 2 side borders to the center. This reduces stress on the pieced seam.

4. Backing and batting should extend at least 2" on each side of the quilt.

Creating a Quilt Sandwich:

1. Press the backing and top to remove all wrinkles.

2. Lay the backing wrong side up on the table.

3. Position the batting over the backing and smooth out all wrinkles.

4. Center the quilt top over the batting leaving a 2" border all around.

5. Pin the layers together with 2" safety pins positioned a handwidth apart. A grapefruit spoon makes inserting the pins easier. Leaving the pins open in the container speeds up the basting on the next quilt.

Basic Quilting Instructions

Hand Quilting:

   Many quilters enjoy the serenity of hand quilting. Because the quilt is handled a great deal, it is important to securely baste the sandwich together. Place the quilt in a hoop and don't forget to hide your knots.

Machine Quilting:

   All the quilts in this book were machine quilted. Some were quilted on a large, free-arm quilting machine and others were quilted on a sewing machine. If you have never machine quilted before, practice on some scraps first.

Straight Line Machine Quilting Tips:

1. Pin baste the layers securely.

2. Set up your sewing machine with a size 80 quilting needle and a walking foot.

3. Experimenting with the decorative stitches on your machine adds interest to your quilt. You do not have to quilt the entire piece with the same stitch. Variety is the spice of life, so have fun trying out stitches you have never used before as well as your favorite stand-bys.

Free Motion Machine Quilting Tips:

1. Pin baste the layers securely.

2. Set up your sewing machine with a spring needle, a quilting foot, and lower the feed dogs.

Basic Mitered Binding

A Perfect Finish:

The binding endures the most stress on a quilt and is usually the first thing to wear out. For this reason, we recommend using a double fold binding.

1. Trim the backing and batting even with the quilt edge.

2. If possible cut strips on the crosswise grain because a little bias in the binding is a Good thing. This is the only place in the quilt where bias is helpful, for it allows the binding to give as it is turned to the back and sewn in place.

3. Strips are usually cut 2½" wide, but check the instructions for your project before cutting.

4. Sew strips end to end to make a long strip sufficient to go all around the quilt plus 4"- 6".

5. With wrong sides together, fold the strip in half lengthwise. Press.

6. Stretch out your hand and place your little finger at the corner of the quilt top. Place the binding where your thumb touches the edge of the quilt. Aligning the edge of the quilt with the raw edges of the binding, pin the binding in place along the first side.

7. Leaving a 2" tail for later use, begin sewing the binding to the quilt with a ¼" seam.

For Mitered Corners:

1. Stop ¼" from the first corner. Leave the needle in the quilt and turn it 90°. Hit the reverse button on your machine and back off the quilt leaving the threads connected.

2. Fold the binding perpendicular to the side you sewed, making a 45° angle. Carefully maintaining the first fold, bring the binding back along the edge to be sewn.

3. Carefully align the edges of the binding with the quilt edge and sew as you did the first side. Repeat this process until you reach the tail left at the beginning. Fold the tail out of the way and sew until you are ¼" from the beginning stitches.

4. Remove the quilt from the machine. Fold the quilt out of the way and match the binding tails together. Carefully sew the binding tails with a ¼" seam. You can do this by hand if you prefer.

Finishing the Binding:

5. Trim the seam to reduce bulk.

6. Finish stitching the binding to the quilt across the join you just sewed.

7. Turn the binding to the back of the quilt. To reduce bulk at the corners, fold the miter in the opposite direction from which it was folded on the front.

8. Hand-sew a Blind stitch on the back of the quilt to secure the binding in place.

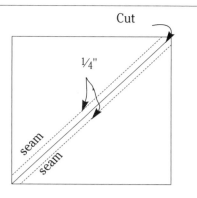

Half-Square Triangle

1. Place 2 squares right sides together.
2. Draw a diagonal line from corner to corner.
3. Stitch ¼" on each side of the line.
4. Cut squares apart on the diagonal line.
5. Open the 2 new squares with 2 colors.
6. Press. Trim off dog-ears.
7. Center and trim to size.

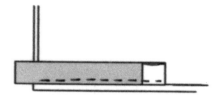

Align the raw edge of the binding with the raw edge of the quilt top. Start about 8" from the corner and go along the first side with a ¼" seam.

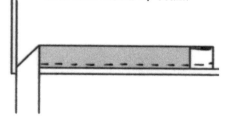

Stop ¼" from the edge. Then stitch a slant to the corner (through both layers of binding)... lift up, then down, as you line up the edge. Fold the binding back.

Align the raw edge again. Continue stitching the next side with a ¼" seam as you sew the binding in place.

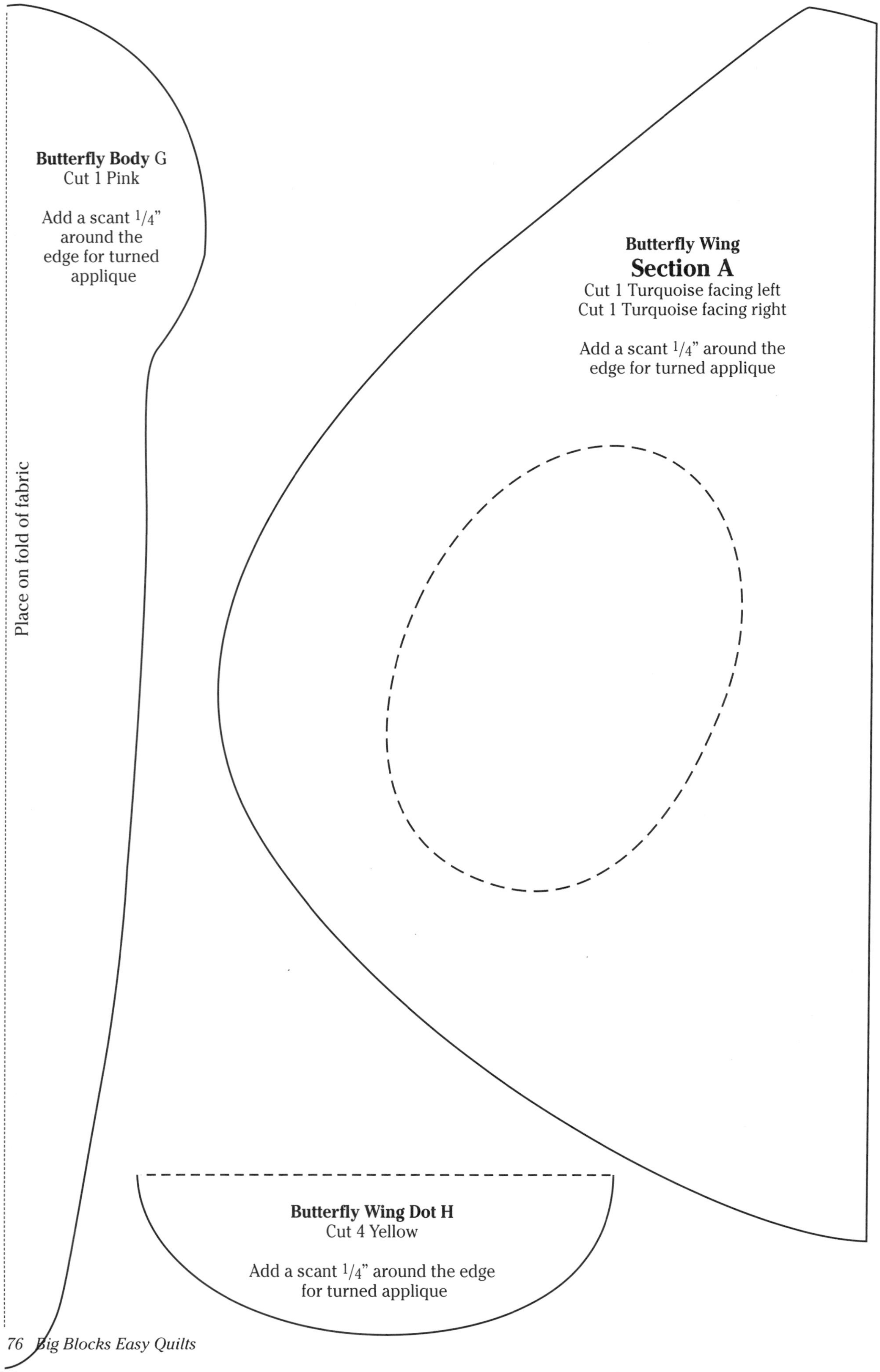

Butterfly Body G
Cut 1 Pink

Add a scant 1/4"
around the
edge for turned
applique

Place on fold of fabric

Butterfly Wing
Section A
Cut 1 Turquoise facing left
Cut 1 Turquoise facing right

Add a scant 1/4" around the
edge for turned applique

Butterfly Wing Dot H
Cut 4 Yellow

Add a scant 1/4" around the edge
for turned applique

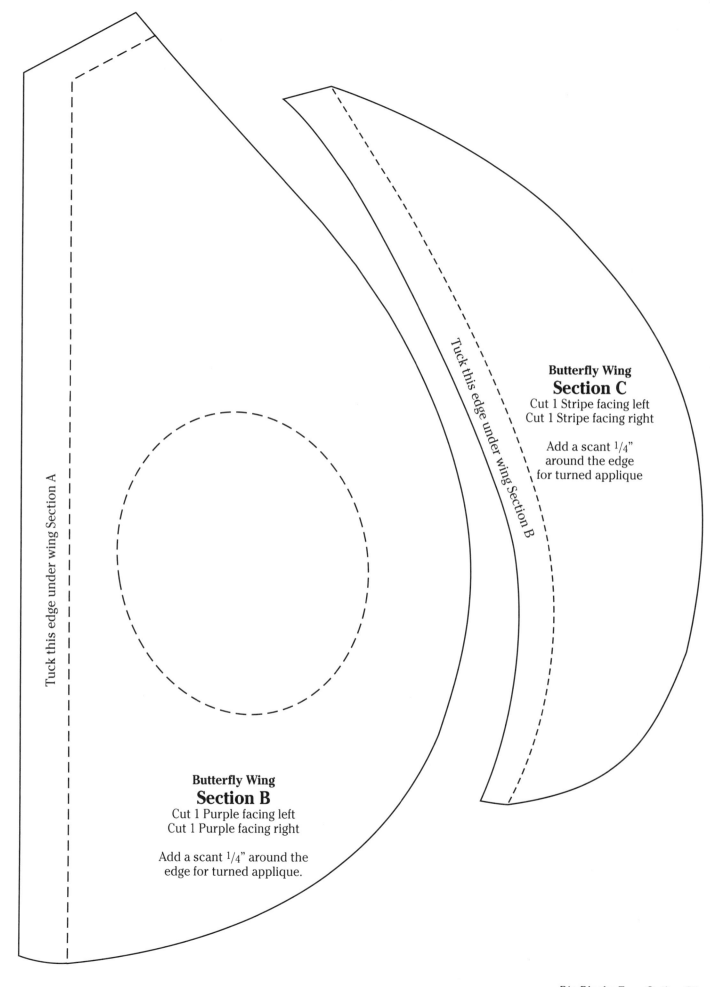

Tuck this edge under wing Section A

Tuck this edge under wing Section B

Butterfly Wing
Section C
Cut 1 Stripe facing left
Cut 1 Stripe facing right

Add a scant $1/4$"
around the edge
for turned applique

Butterfly Wing
Section B
Cut 1 Purple facing left
Cut 1 Purple facing right

Add a scant $1/4$" around the
edge for turned applique.

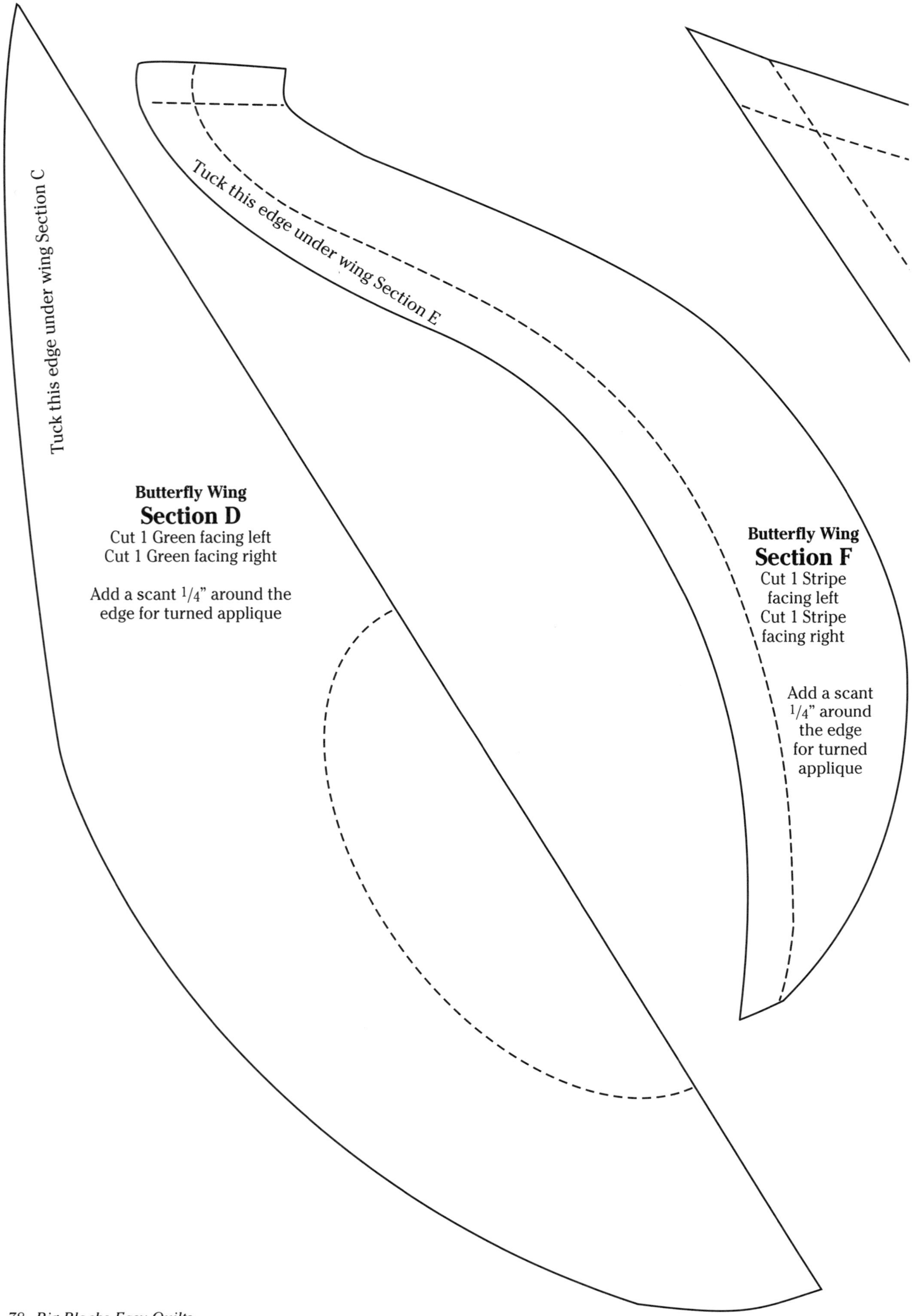

Tuck this edge under wing Section C

Tuck this edge under wing Section E

Butterfly Wing
Section D
Cut 1 Green facing left
Cut 1 Green facing right

Add a scant 1/4" around the
edge for turned applique

Butterfly Wing
Section F
Cut 1 Stripe
facing left
Cut 1 Stripe
facing right

Add a scant
1/4" around
the edge
for turned
applique

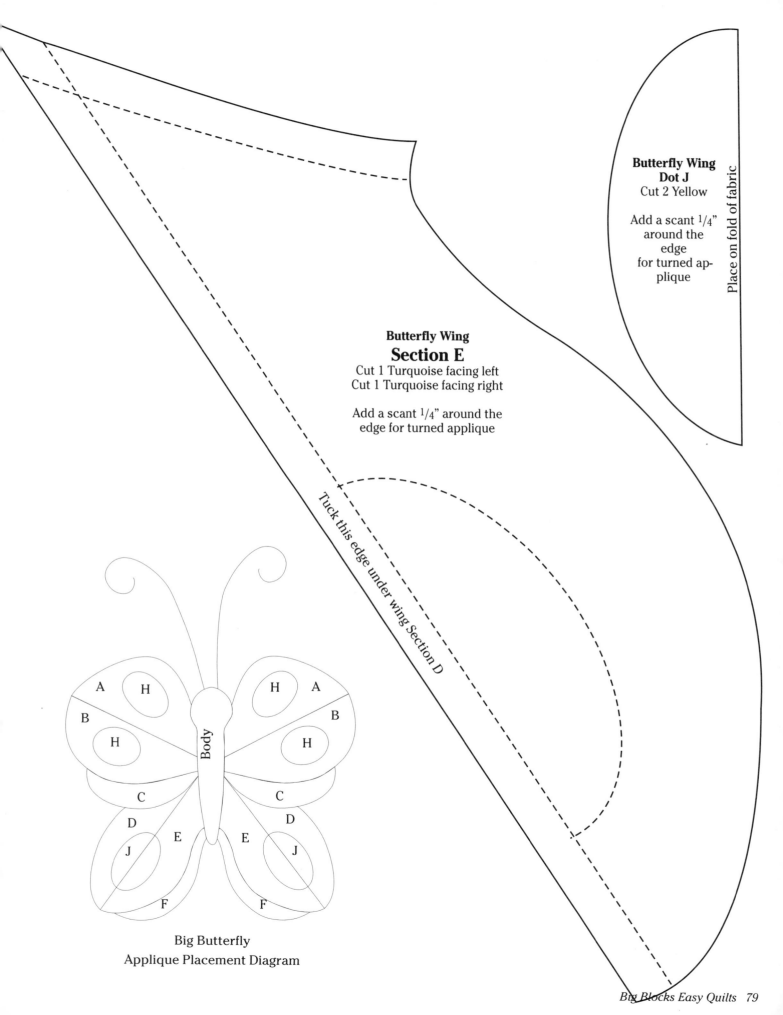

**Butterfly Wing
Dot J**
Cut 2 Yellow

Add a scant 1/4"
around the
edge
for turned ap-
plique

Place on fold of fabric

**Butterfly Wing
Section E**
Cut 1 Turquoise facing left
Cut 1 Turquoise facing right

Add a scant 1/4" around the
edge for turned applique

Tuck this edge under wing Section D

Body

Big Butterfly
Applique Placement Diagram

Big Butterfly

photo is on page 83

SIZE: 68½" x 76½"
TIP: Add more borders to make a larger quilt.

YARDAGE:
Yardage is given for using either fabric yardage or
   'Layer Cake' squares.
We used a *Moda* "Butterfly Fling" by Me & My Sister
   'Layer Cake' collection of 10" x 10" fabric squares
-    we purchased 1 'Layer Cake'

4 squares	OR	⅓ yard White prints
8 squares	OR	⅝ yard Pink
8 squares	OR	⅝ yard Green
8 squares	OR	⅝ yard Purple
7 squares	OR	⅝ yard Blue
4 squares	OR	⅓ yard Yellow

Center & Border #3	Purchase 1⅜ yards White print
Border #4 & Binding	Purchase 2⅙ yards Green
Backing	Purchase 5⅓ yards
Batting	Purchase 77" x 85"

Sewing machine, needle, thread
DMC pearl cotton or 6-ply floss
#22 or #24 chenille needle

PREPARATION FOR SQUARES:
   Cut all squares 10" x 10".
   Label the stacks or pieces as you cut.

SORTING - Sort the following 10" x 10" squares into stacks:

POSITION	QUANTITY & COLOR
Snowball Blocks A	1 Pink, 1 Green, 1 Purple, 1 Blue
Snowball Corners B	2 White
Blocks C	6 Pink, 6 Green
Blocks D	6 Purple, 4 Blue
Cornerstones E	1 Yellow
Appliques	1 Pink, 1 Green, 3 Yellow, 2 Blue, 1 Purple, 1 White stripe

CUTTING:
Tiny Butterfly Appliques:
From 2 Yellow butterfly prints, cut out 9 small butterflies.
We cut out 3 Pink, 3 Blue, 2 Yellow, and 1 Green.

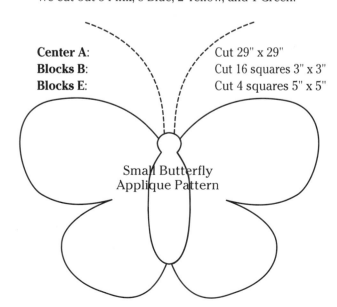

Center A:	Cut 29" x 29"
Blocks B:	Cut 16 squares 3" x 3"
Blocks E:	Cut 4 squares 5" x 5"

Small Butterfly
Applique Pattern

LARGE BUTTERFLY APPLIQUE:
   See Basic Instructions.
   Cut out the pieces from the patterns. Applique as desired.

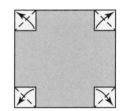
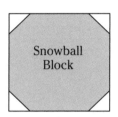

Snowball Block

Snowball Corners Diagram

SNOWBALL BLOCKS A:
   Refer to the Snowball Corners diagram.
   For each block A, align a White square B
     with each corner.
   Draw a diagonal line as shown and sew on
     the line.
   Fold the corner back and press. Repeat
     for all corners.

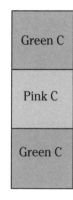

Green C

Pink C

Green C

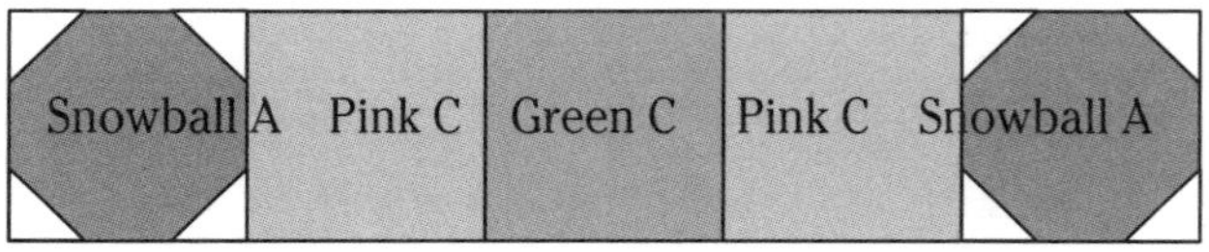

Snowball A   Pink C   Green C   Pink C   Snowball A

BORDERS:
Border #1:
Refer to the Quilt Assembly diagram for block placement and direction.

Side Borders #1
Sew the following block C's together vertically: Green-Pink-Green.
   Press. Make 2.
     Sew one strip-set unit to the left side of the center Butterfly block.
     Sew one strip-set unit to the right side of the center Butterfly block.

Top and Bottom Borders #1
Sew the following block C's together horizontally: Green-Pink-Green.
   Press. Make 2.
     Sew a Snowball Block A to each end of both strip-set units
      (note that the colors will change, refer to the photo).
     Sew one strip-set unit to the top of the center Butterfly block.
     Sew one strip-set unit to the bottom of the center Butterfly block.

E	Purple Block D	Blue Block D	Purple Block D	Blue Block D	Purple Block D	E

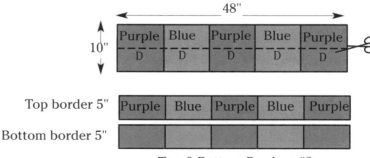

Purple Block D	B Pink Snowball Block A B	Pink Block C	Green Block C	Pink Block C	B Green Snowball Block A B	Purple Block D
Blue Block D	Green Block C		Center		Green Block C	Blue Block D
Purple Block D	Pink Block C				Pink Block C	Purple Block D
Blue Block D	Green Block C				Green Block C	Blue Block D
Purple Block D	B Blue Snowball Block A B	Pink Block C	Green Block C	Pink Block C	B Purple Snowball Block A B	Purple Block D
E	Purple Block D	Blue Block D	Purple Block D	Blue Block D	Purple Block D	E

Big Butterfly - Quilt Assembly Diagram

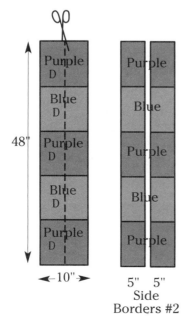

48"

Purple D / Blue D / Purple D / Blue D / Purple D

←10"→

5"   5"
Side
Borders #2

48"

10"

Purple D	Blue D	Purple D	Blue D	Purple D

Top border 5" | Purple | Blue | Purple | Blue | Purple |

Bottom border 5" | | | | | |

Top & Bottom Borders #2

Border #2:
Sides #2:
    Sew the following D squares together end to end:
        Purple-Blue-Purple-Blue-Purple to make a piece 10" x 48". Press.
    Cut the strip in half to make 2 strip-set units, each 5" x 48".
    Sew side borders to the quilt. Press.
Top and Bottom Borders #2:
    Sew the following D squares together end to end:
        Purple-Blue-Purple-Blue-Purple to make a piece 10" x 48". Press.
    Cut the strip in half to make 2 strip-set units, each 5" x 48".
    Sew a White cornerstone E to each end of both strips to make a 5" x 57".
    Sew top and bottom borders to the quilt. Press.

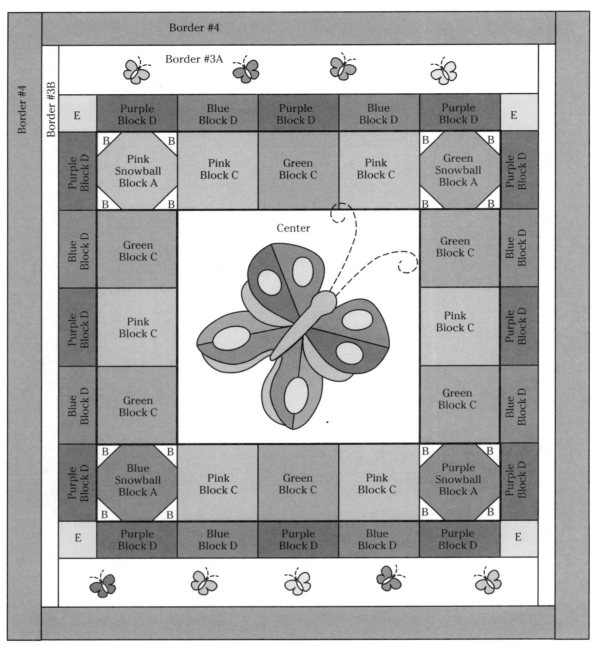

Big Butterfly - Quilt Assembly Diagram

BORDERS:

Border #3:
Sew strips together end to end.
  #3A - Cut 2 White strips 6½" x 57" for top and bottom.
  #3A - Sew top and bottom borders to the quilt. Press.
  #3B - Cut 2 White strips 2½" x 69" for sides.
  #3B - Sew side borders to the quilt. Press.

Outer Border #4:
Cut strips 4½" wide parallel to the selvage to eliminate piecing.
  Cut 2 strips 4½" x 77" for sides.
  Cut 2 strips 4½" x 61" for top and bottom.
  Sew top and bottom borders to the quilt. Press.
  Sew side borders to the quilt. Press.

Butterfly Appliques: See Basic Instructions.
  Applique butterflies in the White center and border.
  Embroider antennae on all butterflies with a long and
    short Running stitch.

FINISHING:

Quilting: See Basic Instructions.
Binding: Cut strips 2½" wide.
  Sew together end to end to equal 302".
  See Binding Instructions.

Suppliers - Most quilt and fabric stores carry an excellent assortment of supplies. If you need something special, ask your local store to contact the following companies.
FABRICS, 'JELLY ROLLS',
'FAT QUARTERS'
  Moda and United Notions,
  Dallas, TX, 972-484-8901

QUILTERS
  Susan Corbett, 817-361-7762
  Julie Lawson, 817-428-5929
  Sue Needle, 817-589-1168

MANY THANKS
to my staff for
their cheerful
help and wonder-
ful ideas!
Kathy Mason
Patty Williams
Donna Kinsey
Janet Long
David & Donna
  Thomason